"We strongly recomm

"The Perfectionist is one of the major le ... ... family of selves that live within each of us. In this book, Cynthia brings clarity as to how the Perfectionist operates, the mischief it can cause in our personality, and, most importantly, she shows us how to deal with our perfectionism in everyday life. This book will serve health care givers as well as the general public, and we strongly recommend it to you."

Hal Stone, Ph.D., and Sidra Stone, Ph.D.
Authors, *Embracing Our Selves* and *Embracing Your Inner Critic*

"Cynthia Curnan brilliantly takes you on a ride through life, examining the Perfectionist vs. Essence. This well-crafted book smooths out the rough spots, which makes the ride so much more pleasant . . . gives the tools to examine the Perfectionist and find a balance to the see-saw of life . . . orchestrates beautifully how to look at both sides and blend them, through inner guidance, into the most delicious Vanilla Swirl ice cream."

Linda Gray
Actor, Director, Producer
United Nations Goodwill Ambassador to U.N.F.P.A.

"In this wonderfully wise and timely book, Dr. Curnan liberates all those who have been taken hostage by the myth of perfection and reminds them that life is not a performance, but a living practice, and it is through our imperfection that we find our true nature and our original voice."

Michael Jones
Composer, Pianist
Author, *Creating an Imaginative Life*

"An important book in its straightforward and creative way of integrating the best concepts of modern psychology with age-old common sense. A powerful yet practical guide to inner healing. A unique book by a unique woman."

Alvin P. Ross, Ph.D.
Founder, Ryokan College

"A wonderfully perceptive and sensitive guide to your own inner truth. Dr. Curnan is the first person I know who talks about getting back to basic instincts and separating them from anxieties."

Eve Roberts
Master Acting Teacher, USC

"No matter who you are, there's something in this book that will open your eyes to parts of yourself you have not yet explored. Cynthia has done an amazing job of self-analysis and has been courageous enough to share it in ways that allow even the most casual reader to gain something from the process."

Channing Dungey
Sr. VP/Film Producer, Material

"I was stuck on a play for ten years. It was the worst case of writer's block I'd ever known. Cynthia's book, *The Care and Feeding of Perfectionists*, helped me build a bridge over the block. Within two days, I had turned a problem play into my most meaningful and successful work ever. I have since used her book as a reference manual in the writing courses I teach. Invaluable resource!"

Jim McGrath
Playwright, Winner of L.A. Theaters' Ovation Award

"Brilliantly insightful, highly practical. Based on core life experiences. Clear, concise examples for patients, clients, students, and therapists. Bold, penetrating catch phrases."

Marvin Portner, M.D.

"This touching and heartfelt book will delight perfectionists and those who love them. Dr. Curnan is one of those rare teachers who walks her talk. I highly recommend it."

William Collinge, Ph.D.
Author, *Subtle Energy:*
Awakening to the Unseen Forces in Our Lives

The Care
and Feeding
of Perfectionists

The Care
and Feeding
of Perfectionists

Cynthia Curnan, Ph.D.

NORTH STAR PUBLICATIONS
Georgetown, Massachusetts

North Star Publications
P. O. Box 10
Georgetown, MA 01833
(978) 352-9976 • fax (978) 352-5586
http://www.RcadersNdex.com/northstar

Cover design: Salwen Studios, Keene, NH
Cover photo: Jim Hagopian—Visual Vibrations

Printed in Canada

Publisher's Cataloging-in-Publication

Curnan, Cynthia.
    The care and feeding of perfectionists / Cynthia Curnan. —
1st ed.
    p. cm.
    Includes bibliographical references and index.
    ISBN: 1-880823-18-7

    1. Perfectionism (Personality trait)   2. Curnan, Cynthia
I. Title.

BF698.35.P47C87 1998   155.2'32
                                                        QBI98–575

For Christopher—my son, my teacher, and so much more.

Contents

Foreword ix

Introduction xiii

1. The Perfectionist Within Us All 1
2. The Backlash, the Backslide, and Other Consequences 13
3. Inner Guidance and Its Impersonators 23
4. Nine Kinds of Perfectionism 37
5. My Life as a Good Girl/Bad Girl 53
6. Challenging My Perfectionism 65
7. When Two Perfectionists Collide 79
8. The Process of Recovery 85
9. Coming Into the Moment 97
10. Calling on the Unconscious 111
11. Perfectionism and Your Career 123
12. True Stories From My Clients 129

Epilogue: A Promise 151
Appendix: An Inner Guidance Course 153
Glossary 165
Bibliography 171
Index 175

Foreword

Cynthia Curnan is a psychotherapist of vision and creativity. More than that, she is an extraordinary woman, thoroughly schooled in psychology and psychotherapy as a science and an art. It is her experience as a searching and growing human being that energizes this book. Dr. Curnan has given us a book about the deep inner human hunger for meaning and health. I read *The Care and Feeding of Perfectionists* with a growing sense that I had never read a book quite like it before.

This book is a mirror reflection of many of us as we search for meaning in our lives. It is a daring revelation of the author's own strengths and weaknesses as a human being. Not many writers have the courage to face themselves in this way—much less to put it down on paper. The book offers important new ways of discovering how humans feel and function, hope and grow, stumble and fall, endeavor and heal.

As the chief administrative officer of a college, a professional training institute for psychotherapists and psychologists, I have been privileged to know and interact with many hundreds of men and women. They come to study and search as they acquire skills and competencies in psychology, so that they may go forth and become healers. Many bring with them serious wounds in need of healing, and through their classes and study groups they become whole. I observe as the passive become assertive, the aggressive become more mellow, the perfectionists slow down and learn to take risks.

In her struggles to achieve her educational goal, Dr. Curnan impressed all about her with her awareness that she had to resolve her own inadequacies, heal her own wounds, before she could hope to help others find balance in their lives. She became a good therapist by listening intently to the known information about humans and humanness from the field of psychology. She overcame her own demons, and dared to become both a learned professional and a unique woman. She found the path that led to becoming whole in mind and spirit.

Her book demonstrates what really takes place within the human spirit when we reach out for growth, balance, and psychological health. The greatest virtue of this very readable book lies in the fact that it does not attempt to overload us with the traditional outlooks and attitudes of psychology. Rather, in its straightforward way it integrates the best concepts of psychology with age-old common sense, as it guides the reader to inner healing.

The Care and Feeding of Perfectionists deserves careful and reflective attention. It will happily reward anyone who is seeking balance in life.

Alvin P. Ross, Ph.D.
Chairman of the Board
Ryokan College

Acknowledgments

To give thanks for the creation of this book, I have to go back to early discoveries regarding my perfectionism. Marshall Summers was the first person to show me that I was a worthwhile person in spite of my imperfections. He ignited my experience of my own inner guidance. He enabled me to see myself more accurately than ever before, and I am eternally grateful to him. Dr. Al and Marcia Ross, the heads of Ryokan College, believed in me at a critical life-shaping point in my life. Drs. Ronald Alexander and Bruce Gregory helped me immeasurably, in both the discovery of and the antidote for my perfectionism. I thank them together, because I think of them both as "The Bringers of the Depths." Their presence inspired, in the very center of my heart, a welcome and sacred personal surrender from perfectionism.

The work of Dru Simms and Chelsea Quinn Yarbro deeply informed me, and opened my eyes to the many ways that fear disguises itself as truth. Their teaching and support allowed me to further open my heart to myself and all human beings. Thanks go to Dr. Susan Flynn for the way she mentored and trusted me during my doctoral process, and for her invaluable mirroring in the earlier years of my studies. Love and gratitude go to Phyliss Shankman for the many roles she played with me in my self-discoveries. Over the years, she was teacher, "Auntie Mame," colleague, and dear friend. Perhaps most of all, she taught me about personal power.

For a much-needed confirmation of what I dared to believe was true, thanks go to "Emmanuel," who teaches us amnesiacs that nothing is wrong, no matter how many spills we take (and cause) along life's way. My deepest devotion goes to Ram Dass for the "Chinese water torture" effect of his message. Since 1975, his words, voice, and presence have penetrated, drip by drip, to become a part of my being. I also thank my editor, Sonia Nordenson, for singlehandedly pulling this book into shape. And finally I thank my Love, who wishes to remain unnamed, for being my gift, the reward for all my hard work, the one who shows me, and shares with me, the glory of life beyond perfectionism.

Introduction

In May of 1994, I went into the African bush with six other women. Every day we walked together silently; each night we sat around a fire and contemplated the day now ending. The trip had a different meaning for each of us. For me, it was a chance to see my relationship to myself, through my experience with the ruggedness of the land and my contact with the other women.

One event defined the trip's meaning for me. We were gathered around the fire on one of our last nights, recalling our experiences and teasing each other. We joked about the ones who had insisted on presenting the hyenas with a tempting nightly buffet, by sleeping outside in a row. One of the women in the circle found a tick in a delicate place, and we all got very involved in tick removal. Another woman danced around the fire, removing the bra that covered her mastectomy scar and throwing it into the flames as we all cheered for her self-celebration.

We talked about how close we felt to nature. So simple and primitive was our trip that we had drunk water out of the ground and swum naked in the streams and pools. We were going on about how good it had felt to let go of our overcivilized selves when one women said, "Just don't try to separate Cynthia from her lipstick and mascara."

My face broke into a release of childish, hysterical laughter. While I was laughing, I had a spontaneous flash of insight. I realized that the comment would have stung me in the past; I would have felt caught and exposed in my vanity. Now, I felt blessed by self-acceptance, and tears came to my eyes. I collapsed into sobbing, convulsive, stomach-muscle-straining laughter. It felt like the shattering of a brittle shell, and it left me feeling soft, naked, pink, and brand-new.

All my life I had been a perfectionist, extremely vain and hard on myself. During that pivotal laughing-crying jag, I released the painful, damaging aspects of my perfectionism and accepted all the rest. I thought, *Now I can be vain and not be hard on myself about it.* I smiled at how ludicrous I was, holding steadfastly to my lipstick and mascara, with six women in the middle of the Kalahari Desert. And then I thought, *But I wear it because I like it. I do it for me, because it makes me feel good.*

This book is not about stripping away perfectionism. It is about sorting through it to find the aspects that hurt us and the ones that can help us. For when we let go of the parts that hurt us, they are replaced by what seem like miracles. This book shares my personal discoveries and those made by my clients as we've worked together in my practice as a psychotherapist. We are happy to share with you our struggles, as well as our celebrations.

In my life, becoming less of a perfectionist and more of a complete person has been a long-term goal. I believe that, even if we are born into less-than-desirable circumstances, we have limitless possibilities. We can begin by turning that inner voice, the one that tells us we aren't good enough, into a tool for self-realization.

It's Thanksgiving Day, and I'm feeling reflective. As I look back over the long process that has led to this moment, waves of gratitude for my own Perfectionist wash over me. I started out thinking the Perfectionist was the best of me, then passed through a time of considering it my enemy. Now I accept it as the one who taught me how to fight, win, surrender, and thrive. My ongoing battles with it have given me the mental, visual, and visceral acuity that come only from feeling oneself to be under siege. Thanks to the Perfectionist in me, I now know that I can meet any challenge life brings.

Perfectionism has its uses. It makes us suffer until we learn compassion, and helps us to master vital skills. And, once in a blue moon, when we hit that ping of perfection, it sure feels good.

1

The Perfectionist
Within Us All

The future is here. Technology has made quantum advances, and continues to progress at a dizzying rate. The world's knowledge is at our collective fingertips; never before has it been possible for an individual to know, to have, and to do so much. And never before has it been so evident that life can be either a splendid or a daunting experience, and that the choice between these extremes is entirely up to us.

"May You Live in Interesting Times"

The quotation above is an old Chinese blessing sometimes found in fortune cookies. It hints of possibilities that spark in us both excitement and a certain dread. The excitement springs from our wildest imagination and deepest heart's desires. The dread arises from the losses we've suffered and seen others incur, from painful memories of past mishaps. Moving toward the excitement causes the dread to gnaw at us. Moving toward the dread feels dreadful. Not moving at all keeps us caught between our hopes and our fears, as life spins away from our grasp.

Certainly we are living in interesting times. This book is for those who feel the excitement and want to follow it wherever it leads, but are still sometimes immobilized by dread. It is for those who, in pushing and racing to stay ahead of the dread, have lost the feeling of excitement and want to get it back. It is for the hungry, the ambitious—the dreamers and idealists hell-bent on making their dreams come true. If you feel more

1

pressure than pleasure in your life . . . if your shoulders are burdened by the needs and wishes of others and you want to unburden yourself to follow your own needs and desires . . . then read on. This book is for you.

A Definition of Perfectionism

If the string of a violin is too tight, it breaks; if it is too loose, it won't play. For me, this stringed-instrument metaphor aptly describes two coexisting aspects of the human psyche. Each part has its own separate thoughts, feelings, motives, and identity. The overly tight part and the part that is too loose are opposites, but they are fused to each other like the flip sides of a coin. Together, they make up a false self that exists in each of us. The loose part feels powerless, and therefore assumes a helpless role. The tight part wants to be all-powerful, and tries to assume a superhuman role. This latter part is perfectionism. To return to the violin metaphor, the Perfectionist is "strung too tightly" in direct response to the "slack" helplessness in the psyche. Both parts are false because, in reality, we are neither helpless nor all-powerful.

The psychological label for perfectionism is *narcissism*, but I find that term disparaging and also inadequate. We tend to think of narcissism only as conceited self-love, and thereby miss the full nature of the predicament. Equating perfectionism with narcissism also prevents us from realizing the universal pervasiveness of perfectionism in the human race.

The psychological term for the helpless part of the psyche that continually seeks rescue is *borderline personality*, but here again the term fails to convey either the challenge faced or the widespread nature of this passive trait.

Perfectionism derives from the ego (or actually, in psychoanalytic theory, from the superego). The ego has different meanings in different systems; its definition varies according to the theory subscribed to. For our purposes, let us say that the ego is, like the body, a useful part of our Earthly equipment, and that the Perfectionist is a component of the ego that *thinks* it is capably negotiating reality in our behalf.

The Perfectionist thrives in that part of the consciousness that is afraid and that wants to go to sleep. Resistance to its acknowledgment is quite natural. It is no easy task to identify and claim the Perfectionist, for it doesn't want to be found out. Besides, who wants to challenge perfectionism before knowing that there is something better?

The Making of a Perfectionist

When I was a child, my mother looked to me to make her feel better. She had high anxiety and low depressive states. She felt helpless to manage her moods, so she sought to regulate them through controlling my behavior. My behavior, then, instead of being natural, was governed by: *Is Mommy in a good mood or a bad mood?*

Helplessness is learned when the personality is not free to develop in harmony with the inner self. This is especially likely when one of a child's primary caretakers is dysfunctional due to alcoholism or another addiction, or even due to chronic illness. Another source of helplessness is the overcontrol brought on by parental fear, which prevents a child from separating and exploring enough to learn self-reliance. The child's repeated efforts to build an individual identity are discouraged by the parent(s), while dependent or compliant behaviors are rewarded. Eventually a sense of futility or dependency replaces the drive toward autonomy. The child essentially gives up trying to grow up.

In addition, parents invariably pass on their own struggle with perfectionism and helplessness to their children. A child copies and often exaggerates the parenting style by which he or she is raised. Thus, the resulting Perfectionist is a frightened child's rendering of a parent. For each one of us, helplessness, like perfectionism, occurs somewhere on a continuum of severity ranging from mild impairment, such as sporadic helplessness in specific areas of injury, to a severe personality disorder that creates permanent incompetence.

When we are in a helpless state, we feel confused and vulnerable. Unable to handle life's challenges, we collapse like a lost child. Rescue is our only hope; we want to be lifted out of our predicament somehow. To the rescue comes the all-powerful Perfectionist part of our personality—throwing us a lifeline, or so it seems. But every rescue has its price. This rescue amounts to the blind (an inflated self-concept) leading the blind (a deflated self-concept). What seemed like salvation becomes a problem in itself, because the deliverance we thought we were getting turns into indentured servitude.

Unable to grow up and take responsibility, we get caught in an endless loop of lofty starts (the push of perfectionism) and backlashes (collapses into helplessness). These backlashes are perceived by the Perfectionist as weakness or a failure of character. After each collapse of a new start, our Perfectionist feels more disdain for our helplessness, and we feel more hopeless. Our internal conversation can go something like this: *No matter how strong a start I make, or how hard I try, I always fail, because I just can't follow through.*

As you can see, the Perfectionist's rescue attempts actually perpetuate the very condition it seeks to eliminate—that collapse into the feeling of helplessness. We give ourselves too much to do, in too little time and with no support, and under these circumstances we cannot win. Any success that we enjoy usually happens in spite of the Perfectionist, not because of it. So, instead of being helped up the mountain by the Perfectionist, we end up having to carry it on our back. To reach the mountaintop—and especially to enjoy the climb—we need to look elsewhere for guidance.

Have You Met Your Own Perfectionist?

Nearly everyone is afflicted by perfectionism to some degree, and it is easy to see it in others. The challenge is to learn to see it in ourselves. Whoever you are, you may be sure that there is a Perfectionist living inside you. In the course of your life so far, this Perfectionist may have failed you and you may have failed it. You may like it or hate it, but it is there to be encountered. Of course, it doesn't want to be encountered; it wants only to be obeyed. But by the time you finish reading this book, you and your Perfectionist will be on intimate terms.

Most of us have selective perfectionism, originating from specific areas of injury. In this form of the problem, compensation continually tries and fails to cancel out an insecurity. If you want to see your Perfectionist, take a look at your relationships. How do you treat other people? How do they treat you? Since we gravitate to people and situations that mirror us, our relationships with others mirror the relationship we have with the self. If we learn to respond to life's challenges from this perspective, we will be able to notice that, as we grow, our outer relationships change to reflect our inner changes. Eventually the Perfectionist will become more manageable and cooperative than before, and our relationships with others will follow suit.

"If the String Is Too Tight, It Breaks; Too Loose, It Won't Play"

Siddhartha, who became the Buddha, heard these words and through them received the wisdom of the Middle Way. Balance and moderation constitute the middle way, which is the best remedy for the predicament of perfectionism and the very thing the Perfectionist dreads. The middle way is an integration, a blending of two extremes. The Perfectionist dreads the middle way because it believes that balance and moderation equal mediocrity.

Though it may at first be a hard idea to accept, we all need to find a way to include our weaknesses rather than exclude them—to own them rather than deny them. You can bridge the extremes of strength and weakness in your own life by conducting a private investigation. Find out how you try too hard, and where you don't try hard enough. Find your middle way by asking questions that activate your inner wisdom. Ask yourself, *Where am I too tight? Where am I too loose? What is my middle way?*

Helpless

When we delve down deeply enough into the Perfectionist, we will find the subpersonality that I call "Helpless" waiting underneath like a kind of vacuous black hole. Everyone's Helpless part is unique, for it holds the core of the specific injury that first evoked the Perfectionist. Mine is a depressed, wounded self that I unknowingly wrote off early in life as too damaged to repair and did not reencounter for many years. I never completely entered this aspect of myself, because my Perfectionist kept me out.

Now that I have ventured to explore my helplessness, I can report that my own form of depression feels like a desolate dead zone. It is the weight I carry, or the gravity I force myself to counteract before I do something. It is the part of me that says from the back of my mind, regardless of what the task may be, *I don't feel like it. Nothing really matters anyway.*

Standing before Helpless's black hole can be emotionally overwhelming, and can tempt us to call on the Perfectionist again for a jump start. But to do this will keep us on the infinity wheel of overdrive followed by eventual collapse back into our particular form of helplessness. If we want to break this cycle, we must attend to Helpless—not all at once, but a little at a time.

Helpless at the Doctor's Office

I used to regress into helplessness when I went to see any medical doctor. I bowed to the doctor's authority and became a child in an adult's body. I felt powerless; I was at the mercy of his expertise. I'd get wobbly if the doctor seemed impatient or hurried—the result of scary childhood experiences with doctors, plus my mother's impatience whenever I needed her time.

When I left the doctor's office, I felt disoriented. Sometimes I got lost on the way home. My Perfectionist got after me for letting a medical checkup affect me this way, and for behaving like a child. I was so unforgiving of myself that I felt doubly beaten. Until I learned how to comfort—instead of punish—the helpless part of myself, each encounter with a doctor was devastating.

Eventually, the process of my recovery from perfectionism led me to a direct confrontation with my Helpless subpersonality. My first real awareness of this aspect of myself came in a dream in which a cat with crushed hindquarters dragged itself to my door. It looked as if it had been run over by a car. I wanted to get away from it, and couldn't bear to watch it because I knew I couldn't save it. Its eyes locked onto mine as if to say, "I don't need you to save me. I need you to see me."

The cat represented the part of myself I had been rejecting because I considered it too damaged . . . beyond help . . . already dead. Through introspection, I realized that it was not my job to save it. I just needed to stay in its presence long enough to see and feel its suffering—my suffering. Gradually I learned that I need to face up to depression, fear, anxiety, or pain whenever they come up, in order to see them for what they are and pass through them. In the past, my response to these unpleasant feelings had been, "Oh no, not you again!" which of course only compounded them. Now I'm learning to welcome (but not wallow in) my negative feelings. I'm learning not to invite them but to accept them if they come on their own.

What Is Your "Black Hole"?

Before we can know what Helpless needs, it is necessary to find out who Helpless is. Set another place at the table for your own form of helplessness. To stand in the presence of the most injured and powerless part of yourself with compassion and without rejection is vitally important, and can be miraculously healing. This admittedly is not easy, but it's even harder when you think you have to do something. Do nothing . . . just be there and hold steady. Facing one's powerlessness feels akin to volunteering to become powerless again. Stepping close enough to depression to really see what it's made of is an act of courage. Daring to look your rescue fantasy straight in the face weakens its hold on you forever. This is an important threshold crossing—one not to be undertaken lightly. Do not attempt to examine your wounds until you feel supported by your inner guidance. When you are ready, compassion and self-acceptance will heal the old injuries so that you can live a fully human life.

Gauging Perfectionism's Intensity

The Perfectionist can range in its behavior from a mild self-critic to an internal annihilator that can never be pleased. The attempt to master it must match the intensity of the perfectionism. If our efforts don't meet the severity of the challenge, the Perfectionist will continue to dominate. One needs to ask, *How distorted is my Perfectionist's view of me? How tight is its grip? How severely does it punish me?*

For example, imagine an intensity scale of one to ten. A person with no perfectionism is at level one on the scale, where errors and flaws are treated realistically and any correction exactly suits the situation. Someone at intensity level two of perfectionism has a somewhat exaggerated perception of both the "crime" and the appropriate "punishment," and so on, up the scale. Once we know how harsh or lenient our Perfectionist is with us, we have sufficient self-knowledge to plan effective interventions with some accuracy. It takes practice, with a generous allowance for trial and error, to determine the intensity of our perfectionism.

My client Samantha was an eight or nine on the scale. It took a year for us to realize that her Perfectionist thought she should die for her imperfections. My attempts to mirror her were inadequate because I could not comprehend the intensity of her self-hate. My interventions didn't touch her depression, except to the extent that she could feel that I cared for her.

Her perfectionism finally cracked open when, one day, after missing a couple of sessions, Samantha declared: "I've decided it's okay to let myself live as a monster." I was stunned, because only then did I realize to what extent I'd missed the intensity of her perfectionism. My client didn't look like a monster. She had never committed monstrous acts. But her perfectionism was so intense that it could not be budged . . . at least not before it was accurately identified.

Samantha was diagnosed with cancer and given a poor prognosis. Through meditation and visualization practices, she surrendered to the inevitability of her death. But when she returned to her doctors, they told her she was free of cancer. She'd had what is called a spontaneous remission, and was now expected to live.

Samantha had entered therapy because her death urge was so strong that she could not come back into life. Yet it had never occurred to me that her Perfectionist could be so harsh as to believe she deserved to die. She got herself off the Perfectionist's hook and began to enter self-acceptance when she decided to allow herself to live as a monster. Because her belief in her monstrousness was too strong for her to try to change it, it was imperative that Samantha reenter life just as she was. Later on, having gained some strength by this act, she could work to change the belief—which indeed she did. She was buoyed by her body's demonstration that the power of her life force was stronger than that of her death urge. This made it obvious, even to her, that the part that wanted her to live was more powerful than the part that wanted her to die.

Even in the most extreme perfectionism, there is usually a healthy part within that wishes us well. But we have to correctly identify our perfectionism and assess its intensity before we can find it.

The Uses of Struggle

The reason Helpless is so convinced of its need to be rescued is because it never learned how to struggle. Whereas the Perfectionist thinks, *If life is easy, something must be wrong*, Helpless thinks that if life *isn't* easy, something must be wrong. So, before we can transform the Perfectionist, we need to find a way to awaken and activate the dormant struggler in Helpless.

A teacher of mine once said, "The struggler is the best part of a person. It's the hero on the hero's journey who slays the dragon that guards the castle, and wins the princess."

Frustration, the major obstacle to struggle, must be managed to prevent it from ruining our efforts. Among my clients, those who have the most difficulty sustaining their progress are those who can't tolerate frustration. They take it as a signal that they should give up. When we come up against frustration, we have to make a deep inner inquiry to distinguish whether the Perfectionist is pushing or Helpless is resisting. If we persevere and keep asking for guidance, the natural wisdom in us will surface.

One night I had another cat dream, one that gave me insight about my own tendency to struggle unnecessarily. In the dream, I had just awakened when an orange cat jumped on my bed and sang in a rich baritone, "It's so easy." A wall in my room opened, revealing The Land of Easy. People danced and sang "It's so easy" all over the land. As I joined them in the dancing and singing, I experienced how easy life is when I flow with it and allow it to be just as it is. My body felt no gravity, no hindrance to pleasure and grace. The air felt like silk against my movements.

And then I started to push and control. The Perfectionist had weaseled itself into my experience, making it heavy and difficult again. The song slowed as if powered by a dying battery. The air thickened until I could no longer move through it. I realized what I had done, and quit pushing. Instantly, lightness returned to my movements and the ease of the land was restored.

The feeling of this dream was so visceral—and is still so strong in my memory—that it serves as my criterion whenever I start to get caught in excessive effort. The dream taught me how to feel the difference between joyous activity and unnecessary struggle. When we invite guidance and then stay open to receive it, our own inner wisdom gives us directives, such as this dream, in a form that is exactly right for us.

You Can Reinvent Your Life and Career

Prepare to be surprised. Many of the ways you have felt misunderstood by others are ways that you have misunderstand yourself, that you and your Perfectionist have misunderstood each other. Prepare to view yourself in a new light, to see yourself more accurately than ever before. If you desire to live free, beyond the rules and boundaries that now confine you, then it is necessary to learn the fine points of the rules that run you, to know where your boundary lines are currently set. These are limitations imposed by the mind; they do not inherently exist in the world.

If you feel intimidated by the life you really want, join the club. Most of us feel like that, but in deference to the Perfectionist's image requirements we don't usually admit it. I'll let you in on a secret I've learned over the years: most growth-oriented people feel as if they're "in over their heads"; nearly all high achievers feel like charlatans.

So I encourage you to set aside your trepidation and think instead of the career opportunities that are out there waiting. A lot of them can't be found in the classifieds, on the career aptitude tests, or listed on the boards of job counseling centers, because many of these careers are still in the making. They are gestating within someone's imagination (perhaps yours), waiting to be given form. Many of the people working in new fields of endeavor are making it up as they go along—even they don't yet fully know what they're doing. Once they have it down, it may be time to try something else.

One important difference between people who successfully pioneer new careers and those who fall behind is the ability to endure the inevitable learning curve. As Buckminster Fuller said, "To learn something new takes a minimum of 20 percent mistakes and an optimum of 38 percent mistakes." In order to risk making those necessary mistakes, we have to outsmart the Perfectionist.

For you, it may or may not be time to begin a whole new career. Maybe it's time to expand on your current occupation. More and more companies are giving employees latitude to run with new ideas. Think of all the ideas you've had that you knew were good ones. Yet something stopped you from speaking up or following through. Encourage your ideas; learn what has blocked them. If you have, or want to have, a vision or a sense of mission, it is essential to seek out the nature of your personal predicament. That way, you won't have to wake up one day wondering, *Where did my life go?*

A Starting Place

Begin by remembering all that you have ever wanted to be, do, and have—what you have yearned to give, share, and receive. Let these recollections take any form or start out completely formless. Let them come as feelings, as images, as a rediscovery of lost dreams. Call up from the deepest places within you every forgotten or pushed-away ambition. Gather these in without judging them as too big or too small.

If the feeling of dread also starts to arise, let it do so; it has to present itself before it can be dismantled. Let it surface, even if it comes as the memory of all your disappointments, and in your mind's eye push it over to one side while you continue to remember every item on your wish list.

Imagine yourself reorganizing your closet, home, office, career. Call it spring cleaning, remodeling—whatever best serves as your metaphor for throwing out the obsolete, welcoming the new, and restrategizing the rest of your life. Remember, from all your past reorganizations, how everything gets messier when you first begin, and be assured that order will come from this chaos. A painter begins a new work by establishing the space upon which to create it. If you want your life to be an original work of art, then you have some clearing to do in order to prepare this space.

Your Journey of Discovery

In continuing to read this book, you are about to embark on a journey of discovery. On this journey, you will delve more deeply than ever before to discover what it is that you want to achieve in your life. The journey will give you a realization of the resources you already have at your disposal, as well as the ones you don't yet know about. It will disclose to you the real (not imagined) obstacles in your way. Once these are known, they will cease to be insurmountable. Native Americans kept secret the real names of their tribes, for they believed that if their enemies knew their names, they could take away their power. As we name the factors that oppose your efforts, and look them straight in the face, you will be able to seize their power and use it to fortify the new life you are building for yourself.

Whatever it is that you dream of achieving, if some small part of you is willing to go for it, that is the only necessary prerequisite to using this book as your tool, your inspiration, your support system—to go just as far as you dare. The only limits will be the ones that you yourself impose. And if this prospect doesn't scare you as much as it thrills you, you haven't yet dreamed big enough!

2

The Backlash, the Backslide, and Other Consequences

No matter how perfectionism manifests, it always has its cost and its consequences. In this chapter, we will look at some of the undesirable by-products of the problem, and also consider the great importance of self-acceptance in throwing off the Perfectionist's control.

Negative Personal Traits

I have learned as much about perfectionism from my clients as I have from my own process. When individuals come into my office, their Perfectionist is usually acting as the gatekeeper to their real self. They typically exhibit an anxiety that reflects their very sincere attempt to be "good" in their therapy. Of course, their wish to "do it right" only gets in their way. Ironically, this moment that they think they need the Perfectionist most is the moment they need it least. But as usual the Perfectionist prevails, showing itself in their body language, their facial expressions, and the words they choose.

Clients' faces may be taut, strained, or masked with a hollow smile or deliberate expression of "niceness." There is a look and feeling that they are holding themselves together, or presenting themselves correctly. They may avoid looking at me, or look at me not to make contact but to read my response to them. Sometimes I feel a plea from their eyes, as if they are silently asking me to like them.

Their posture can be posed, rigid, or incongruent with their language and facial expression—hands or feet in motion to release anxiety, for instance. Their speech often has a measured rhythm or forceful inflection, and may be fast-paced so as to not waste time or not let their deeper feelings gain on them. The words they choose include "never," "always," "should." The overall feeling is one of control and self-consciousness; they seem unnatural.

Those of my clients who have the most acute perfectionism think of themselves as procrastinators or as lazy, inferior beings. "Doing" is what they most value, yet their perfectionism is so severe that they can't do anything. Their Perfectionist is braced to attack the moment they peek out of their hiding place. They can't make a move, because that very first move wouldn't be good enough. They can't learn anything new, because they're unable to make a perfect beginning. They can neither start nor finish anything, so they withdraw, and succumb to depression.

Once I had an exercise teacher who told me that I put seventy pounds of effort into a ten-pound exercise. When I experienced the truth of her words, I was greatly relieved to know that I could now lighten up. My clients, too, feel this relief, once they learn to identify their perfectionism. Together, we proceed one by one through their many well-fortified defenses, until the Perfectionist feels safe enough to let us see the human behind it.

Blind Spots

One way for us to see our perfectionism is to notice our level of self-consciousness. A child's true nature is not self-conscious. It just is. But if our "isness" was not accepted by our parents, we adapted ourselves to conform to their standards. We did this in order to win love and avoid rejection and pain. We did whatever was necessary to be what our parents wanted us to be. We forgot our original self, and came to believe that we really were our learned behavior. Some of us, in a vain attempt to be free, later become what they *didn't* want us to be—another departure from our true nature.

Parents do the best they can, and seldom know when they are misguiding their children. My mother certainly did a better job with me than her own parents had done with her. And I tried to do a better job with my son than my mother had done with me. But much of my mother's and my behavior was misguided because we were still so wounded and confused by our own childhood experiences.

The vast majority of parents do not abuse their children. But we do pass on our blind spots. Unknowingly, we may want our children to think, feel, and live as we do, or to improve on our behavior and correct the mistakes we made.

When I was raising Chris, I certainly made my share of mistakes. I knew little about the kind of impression I was making on him, or that this would form his particular brand of perfectionism as he grew. I watched his naturally sweet and open self become imprinted with the insecurities that I inadvertently passed on to him. I was trying to give him what my mother hadn't given me, and trying not to give him the complexes I had taken on from Mom.

Many of my errors were sins of omission. I managed to avoid giving Chris some of the harmful influences my mother had given me, but I didn't give him enough of what he needed. My blind spot was my need to be "not my mother"—an imperative that prevented me from being natural with my son and prevented me from clearly seeing his needs.

As a child, my mother felt deprived of love, and consequently she was unable to show me much affection. I in turn felt deprived of love, and later was limited in the love I could express to my son. When I tried to be affectionate with Chris and tell him that l loved him, I was forced and unnatural. He sensed this, and felt uncertain about my love for him.

Internal Conflict

Many of us face an obstacle course of internal conflict from the way we were mirrored in childhood. My mother's continual message to me became mine to my son: *Don't bother me. Can't you see I'm just barely hanging on?* Another pervasive message was: *Don't be who you are. Be who I want you to be.* These parental messages are the mirrors that show our children who they are. If they cause the young person to reject his or her true nature, they result in habits, beliefs, attitudes, and false images that, until they are dismantled, will have a crippling effect.

To untangle internal conflict, we need to notice the distinctly different and divided parts of our psyche. We will usually find one subpersonality that is harsh or mean. Another feels overly indulgent or permissive. Still another feels kind and compassionate. Once found, these need to be differentiated so that we can begin to know which parts to trust and follow.

This process gradually leads to the experience of Inner Guidance, which is kind and respectful even as it reveals an error. This guidance has wisdom, benevolence, and limitless patience. There are many ways to access Inner Guidance; I will discuss some of them in Chapter Three.

The Backlash

In order to meet the Perfectionist's standards and deadlines, we adopt striving behaviors to counter all obstacles. These striving behaviors override self-care needs, and sooner or later result in a collapse of some kind. This collapse or breakdown is the inevitable backlash that follows the Perfectionist's push over the edge.

The Backlash is Helpless behavior, at the utmost opposite of the Perfectionist's most extreme behavior. It ranges from sloth, overeating, or chronic complaining to exhaustion, depression, or illness. The Perfectionist drives us so far out of balance that we have to slingshot backward to restore equilibrium.

In this context, addiction is part of the Backlash, or an attempt to stave it off. I might drink too much coffee and not give myself enough sleep or exercise in order to keep to my writing schedule, which can push me into an episode of chronic fatigue that causes me to lose even more writing time while I'm recovering.

The Perfectionist meets us at the Backlash with a demoralizing running commentary about failure. Mine relishes telling me every painful detail of what I'm doing wrong. First it pushes me to the breaking point, saying, *Keep going, don't stop, drink more coffee, work a little longer, be strong.* Then, when I run out of gas and can't write the next day, it condemns me for breaking down, telling me, *See, you're weak.*

Our work is not to fight the Backlash, nor to fight the Perfectionist, but to wake up again and again from forgetfulness. Backlashes naturally diminish in intensity when we learn to curb the Perfectionist before too much damage is done. As Ram Dass has said, what begins as the daunting "monster in the closet," with self-work becomes the manageable "pest on the shoulder."

The Backslide

The Backslide is that pull toward unconsciousness that exists in all humans, to distract us and lull us back to sleep. It is a kind of gravity that pulls us back to old, familiar ways, causing amnesia, limiting our potential, and reversing hard-won growth. For instance, say I have a specific habit or behavior that I give up, because I think I've finally learned that it's bad for me. Then I forget why I chose to give up the habit, and I start to slip back. An internal voice says, *Why not do what you want? You enjoy it.* I think, *Yeah, what's it gonna hurt?* and I start the behavior all over again.

New Year resolutions usually begin with full force, encounter resistance, and then fizzle out. The resistance is what I call the Backslide. Attempts to stave it off only increase its pull. As a pilot has to factor into a flight plan the degree to which wind resistance affects the speed of travel, the Backslide must be factored into the growth process.

The Backslide dynamic is known by many descriptives, such as "growth versus the status quo," or "the life force versus the death urge." It is the tension between that part of us that wants to awaken and that part that wants to stay asleep.

Here's a typical example of the Backslide in action. My client Alice wanted to go on a healthful diet. She said she was finally ready to treat her body better and lose weight. But she was in hurry, and she started too strictly. She soon felt food cravings, began forgetting why she wanted to remain on the diet, and gradually slipped back to her old eating habits. When she realized what had happened, she became angry with herself for failing.

Alice's Perfectionist had put her on too strict a diet, and had failed to consider the Backslide. The Perfectionist denies this dynamic as a fact of life. When the Backslide exerts its pull, the Perfectionist blames weak will and says, *Just try harder.* If Alice had tried harder, she would have increased the regressive pull. The Backslide is the continual tug of war between the Perfectionist and Helpless. The Perfectionist told Alice, *You must lose weight.* Helpless said, *I can't do it.* This conflict took up so much of Alice's attention and energy that, almost without noticing, she regained the weight she had lost.

Whenever we attempt to make a change for the better, Helpless and the Perfectionist will infiltrate our process. Their struggle opposes our attempts to improve, and has to be factored into the plan. In Alice's case, the solution was for her to go more deeply into herself to find the motivation and support to treat her body better. She needed to notice when the Perfectionist was trying to direct her diet, because the diet would then become too strict for her to follow. Her problem was not a weak will, but an ignorance of the fact that natural forces act against every forward motion.

The challenge for all of us is to respect the power of the Backslide, to see it as a natural part of being human, and to maintain a self-respectful attitude in the face of all opposition. No one argues with gravity. We must remind ourselves again and again that nothing is wrong, even when the Backslide is seemingly winning. We need only wait until the pull peters out—which it eventually does—and then move forward again, without wasting energy lamenting over lost ground.

The Mind-Body Connection

Fear causes perfectionism. When the Perfectionist leads us, it is fear we are following—fear disguised as rightfulness. It took me a long time to recognize those times when fear was controlling me, because I rarely felt identifiable fear. I felt an intense need to know the deeper truth of things, and I considered that an admirable quality. I felt out of control and needed more certainty. These are fearful states that cause the Perfectionist to jump in with seeming conviction and authority. *Follow me*, it says. *I know.* But if we do follow, there are consequences.

When we follow fear, we see ourselves and our world through fear's eyes, and we think fear's thoughts. If my fear is turned inward, something is always wrong with me. If the fear is turned outward, something is wrong with everyone else. We all want love, but if something is always wrong with either me or you, how can we have it? My Perfectionist caused me to live under the continual threat of depression. The struggle to right the wrongs is depressing because it's impossible. To sustain a continual, driven effort to correct our wrongs drives us to grasp for help, and help comes in the form of drugs, alcohol, and other addictions.

The Perfectionist's fear pushes us into addictions by driving us too far for too long. Addictions, then, are misguided attempts to restore a sense of balance and well-being. We need immediate relief and support to keep going. We use our addictions to feel good because the Perfectionist's fear makes us feel so bad.

When we follow fear, we trigger and overstimulate the psychological and physiological effects that accompany fear: anxiety, shallow breathing, adrenaline rushes, a rapid pulse, a racing mind, an upset stomach, and so on. If these effects persist over a long period of time, they erode our health.

Researchers are learning that thought processes and emotional affects cannot be separated from physical functioning. The mind and the body are inextricably connected. There is also mounting medical evidence to show that people worry themselves sick. I have personally observed that, if the Perfectionist maintains control for too long, the immune system becomes weak. The body cannot indefinitely sustain the strain of fearful thinking. If we follow a fearful mind, we transmit fear throughout the physical system, perhaps pushing the body to the brink of disease.

Psychoneuroimmunology

Psychoneuroimmunology (PNI) is a new science that has been pioneered by scientists, medical researchers, and practitioners of mind-body medicine. It postulates that we express our thoughts, feelings, and personality through our brain and nervous system, which affects our immunological defenses and, through them, our general health and well-being. The body, mind, and spirit are interdependent. If any one of these is weak in an individual, that person falls out of balance.

This hypothesis represents a rediscovery of what much of the human race has believed, based on empirical research, throughout recorded history. The Western world lost much of this age-old perspective with the advent of the mechanistic approach to science and medicine that began in the 18th century. In deference to the logical mind, knowledge of the value of emotional and spiritual well-being was driven underground. This state of affairs gave further rise to the Perfectionist, which values the logical mind over all else. Mankind needed scientific breakthroughs to save lives, but the cost was a loss of the spirit of healing.

A triune balance of body, mind, and spirit is necessary for health and well-being. The disruption of this interdependent relationship, even in the name of healing, causes "dis-ease," which may begin in the body, the mind, or the spirit. A disease that begins in one affects the others.

When we resist the seduction of fearfulness and maintain an open mind, great strides toward freedom can be made. The Perfectionist stands at the entryway to our true nature, and its power diminishes when we turn our attention beyond it. When we decline to look to the Perfectionist for guidance, what we find is our own essence, waiting within us to be noticed. Once we have made contact with this essence, we can begin to relinquish our reliance on addictions for relief and support.

The Ineffectiveness of Coercion

Over the years, I have tried to change many things about myself. I have strived to be more disciplined and organized, to keep my car washed and my body toned. I have made an effort to routinely floss my teeth, to eat more vegetables and less fat. These changes always entailed a lot of struggle. Even if I could initiate new behavior, I couldn't persevere in it. Eventually I began to look into my resistance and examine my motives.

My resistance is the part of me that says, *I just don' wanna. Leave me alone.* My motives say, *You're a bad person if you don't.* The result is a battle of wills: *You have to!* followed by, *No I don't, and you can't make me!* The force that wants change may be powerful enough to get me to try really hard, but it's not powerful enough to get me to follow through. I can't possibly summon enough energy to make and hold a change, just to avoid feeling bad—that's too small a payoff for such a big struggle.

The Perfectionist tells me I'm bad if I don't change. It also tells me it doubts that I *can* change, and ridicules me through my efforts instead of offering support. The whole atmosphere is one of self-rejection. My refusal to comply with this kind of internal bullying is only practical, because change won't hold if it's forced.

Because lasting change can't be motivated by self-rejection, we need to remove the "have to" hook. Nobody wants to conform on demand. Change must come from self-acceptance, which is not easy to come by. Strong internal forces oppose it, and we must wade through these to clear the way.

Before making any change, we have to know who wants it, and for what purpose. If I want my car clean because I fear people will think less of me if it's dirty, that motive won't get me to clean my car. The part of me that already feels rejected will be my silent resistance that will reject them back: *If they don't like me, too bad for them!* The Perfectionist needs me to clean up my act and look good. I resent the put-down, and refuse to comply. The car stays dirty, but the Perfectionist succeeds in making me feel crummy about it. If I want my car clean because it gives me pleasure, then that's different. I can probably summon up the time and energy for a self-giving, life-enhancing act.

If I have to eat my vegetables because I still hear my mother screaming at me to sit at the table until they're eaten, the part of me that feels rejected will silently say, *Up yours, Mom. You can't make me.* But if I'm eating vegetables to be healthy and to keep my digestion running smoothly, then I'll probably get those veggies down. The will to do positive things shows up when you're internally guided and supported in a manner that says, *I like you enough to want to help you feel better.*

How Self-Acceptance Leads to Positive Change

Who wants to have to perform in order to be worthy of self-love or to avoid self-rejection? Refuse to cooperate with intimidation tactics, even if they come from yourself. If we want something better for ourselves, we'll have to treat ourselves more nicely to get it.

Our inner wisdom will give us the changes we really want, with no strings attached. We know that a prompting is coming from our true nature when—whatever the challenge may be—we believe we can do it. We know that we are responding to genuine guidance when we feel an upsurge of our own strength, will, and courage while preparing to take action.

Self-acceptance is not self-indulgence. When we turn over a dilemma to our inner awareness, we are not coddled but given a clear assessment of the predicament, and guided in a realistic, step-by-step process toward lasting change. Aliveness, energy, motivation, and inspiration exist only in an atmosphere of self-acceptance. Our efforts to change must be supported by a wish for better self-care. They cannot be makeovers based on self-denigration.

My clients really fight me on this one. It is very hard to let go of the seemingly almighty demand to change. They fear becoming fat, ugly, inert messes if they are easy on themselves for a moment. Earlier in my life I owned a beauty salon. When I did client makeovers, the women often thought their lives would improve if they could achieve the right look. Yet it was their self-rejection, not their appearance, that was hurting their lives.

I'm not saying that there has to be complete self-approval before any changes are initiated. But there is a part inside every one of us that does care. We can find that part and go into it, no matter how small it is. We can nurture it and expand it, and then let it direct the changes. Curiosity and a willingness to identify the Perfectionist and separate it from the deeper voice of wisdom make all the difference. And, in the process of the identification and separation, we may begin to discover qualities of the Perfectionist that can be put to good use.

3

Inner Guidance
and Its Impersonators

Throughout time, many great teachers have taught that each of us is created with an essence, or an innate identity. Zen Buddhists call it original face. It contains empty spaces that are filled with our life experiences, and those experiences either strengthen or weaken the original essence. If we want to feel our most natural self and make the most of life, it is this essence to which we can turn our attention.

Each person has a unique way of thinking about this concept I call Essence. Call it soul, higher self, truest deepest self—whatever we call it, it makes us more than our personality. The personality may clearly reflect this essence, allowing it to shine through, or it may conceal the essence almost entirely.

Acknowledging Our Own Wisdom

The connection with Essence and receptivity to its communications is what I call Inner Guidance, which feels like a deeper knowing. Whether they think of it as intuition, inner truth, or a gut feeling, most people are aware of the part of them that steers them toward their wisest choices. The guidance is an internal experience that has a calming and centering effect. Because this guidance comes from Essence, it is unafraid, no matter what is occurring.

Essence dwells deeper than pain, problems, and the confusion of circumstances. It brings clarity and the feeling of flow that exists behind conflicts. It can be mental, coming through thoughts, or intuitive, coming through insights that slip into awareness in the spaces between thoughts. These have a lighter feel inside the head than ordinary thoughts, as if they are full of helium. Or the guidance can be emotional or inspirational, capturing our attention through subtle or dramatic changes in the feelings. It is wise not to ignore these promptings. How many times have you heard yourself and others say, "I knew it! But I didn't listen."

Inner Guidance can be physical, like felt senses in the body, internal shaking, or noticing that you want to steer the car on a different route to work, though you don't know why. It can come through dreams, visions, or a spiritual experience. Many receive Inner Guidance visually, either through their mind's eye (in pictures or little vignettes) or by looking at beauty and being in the presence of nature. Everyone receives guidance in a different way. Siddhartha received it from the river. Gandhi called it his inner "Voice of Truth." I have received guidance by overhearing a conversation at the table next to me, in a restaurant. The words I heard were my answer to a difficult decision I had to make.

The more we remain alert to the many ways that we can receive our deepest truths, the easier it becomes to distinguish true guidance from false. I find that the state most conducive to accessing Inner Guidance is a neutral one. The neutral state allows us to view both sides of the picture simultaneously. When we're feeling good, we tend to forget the bad: *That's all behind me now.* When we're feeling bad, we tend to forget the good: *I thought I was past this. Now it's going to be bad again forever.* Neutrality allows us to remember that neither the good feeling nor the bad feeling is going to last.

Inner Guidance in Daily Life

Inner Guidance is an abiding internal support system, available every moment. It holds up under the scrutiny of examination, and it holds *us* up when we are challenged by the rigors of life. To reach it, or to let it reach us, it is important to identify and deactivate our self-interference—that combination of perfectionism and helplessness that is unique to each individual.

The Perfectionist is battle-ready at the first sign of a problem, and jumps in to help. It doesn't try to access Inner Guidance, because it already knows what to do. It pushes toward its predetermined solution with an unhesitating overkill approach. Helpless tends to be too self-indulgent or too insufficiently motivated to listen to Inner Guidance. Its self-interference says, *Leave me alone, I don't feel like paying attention. Somebody come and help me.*

When the Perfectionist controls my thoughts and feelings, I feel bad about myself or about somebody else. I feel anxious and urgent. Inner Guidance brings a completely different set of sensations that allow me to feel open, awake, and keenly aware. My experiences in that state can be anything from sobering to inspiring.

The Perfectionist treats little problems as emergencies. Our emotions tell us that something terrible is happening, when actually we are experiencing small problems that contain elements of big problems from the past. Inner Guidance allows us to distinguish small problems from big ones. We learn to separate the present from the past, and to stay aware of the tendency to let unhealed emotional wounds distort reality. We can practice on the easy things first, as we develop the skill of receiving Inner Guidance.

Listening Within

When uncovering our perfectionism, the work is not to get answers but to ask questions. So we need to know what questions to ask. Asking, *Why am I so stupid?* merely invites the Perfectionist's opinions. "Why" questions, in general, inhibit Inner Guidance by confining the inquiry to analytical process. Tapping into Inner Guidance requires the activation of unconscious processes, through asking open-ended questions: *What can I know about this now? Please give me support, strength, and courage. What do I need? Please show me what I can't see.*

After your request is made, listen receptively and with rapt attention, as if waiting to hear a pin drop. If the response is not forthcoming in the time set aside to listen, it is fine to move on through the day, letting the request fall to the back of your mind but checking in every so often to keep the connection open. There can be no sense of demand or desperation in the request. Demand comes from the Perfectionist, and desperation is just Helpless begging to be rescued. It is useful to create a state of wonder and anticipation, not expectation.

Ready to Throw a Tantrum

Here is an example of my own Inner Guidance process. One day I was in a department store, waiting to make a purchase. There were two salespeople, and I was the only customer waiting. One clerk turned to help a woman who had arrived after me. I said nothing, but felt slighted. Then the second salesperson started to help another newcomer.

This felt like an emergency to me. The Helpless aspect of me wanted to cry, while the Perfectionist wanted to yell at the saleswomen for their incompetence. Beyond that, I was angry with myself that something so minor had so rattled me (the Perfectionist again). But since I had made up my mind to distinguish small problems from emergencies, I took this as an opportunity to practice using my Inner Guidance.

First, I had to separate what I needed from what I didn't need. I didn't need the Perfectionist's anger to be directed either toward me or toward the other individuals. I did need mirroring, and compassion from myself for my hurt feelings. I said to myself, *This really hurts. What do I need to do?* My respectful self-questioning activated my Inner Guidance, which then supported me in telling the second clerk—in a manner fitting the situation—that it was my turn.

A Magnitude 2 or a Magnitude 8?

That done, I became curious about my reaction. *What does this remind me of?* I wondered. A memory came to me, of when I was nine years old and on my way to the dentist. My mother always gave me fifteen cents to ride the cable car, but I used the money to buy ice cream instead. I would run down the street, pretending to race the cable car to the ice cream store.

I learned to dread buying my ice cream because I was usually overlooked by the clerks. They only noticed the bigger people, and I was too shy to speak up. I waited in misery until someone saw me, and sometimes I left with no ice cream, feeling humiliated. Even when I was nine, my Perfectionist was furious with me for being so weak, which of course further weakened me. Now, in the department store, I had needed to process my "emergency feeling" so my response could be appropriate to the situation. The nine-year-old's pain needed to be acknowledged as real and then separated from what was happening now.

A small problem in the present can activate a memory of a past injury, but we need to remember that the injury is not happening now. A teacher of mine once said, "It's really an earthquake, but it's only a 2 on the Richter scale. You're feeling an 8 because a 6 is unresolved from your past." When we confuse past experiences with present circumstances, we obscure our Inner Guidance and set up a damaging stress reaction in the body.

The Perfectionist's Heavy Hand

I have to continually check within myself to feel the difference between perfectionism and Essence—to really sense the different experiences inside my body. When I am tapped into Inner Guidance, it is as if there is a compassionate hand on my shoulder. I feel infused with internal support. If I am about to do something new, I feel eager. My heart and mind feel open and ready.

When my perfectionism engages, I feel a weight on my shoulder. My body feels tight. If I am about to try something new, I feel anxious. I may want to go to sleep, or eat something comforting—just to escape the bad feelings. My Perfectionist looks at me and the whole world through a darkly tinted lens. Its position is: *Something is wrong somewhere, and it's my job to find it and make it right.* When I am about to start something new, my Perfectionist says: *Something's going to go wrong.* This doesn't leave much room for the mistakes that are part of any new learning, but then my Perfectionist doesn't permit mistakes. It thinks I should already know what I'm doing.

Essence recognizes the value of miscalculations in the learning process. One of my teachers once said, as I was reeling from an error, "To master anything takes one thousand mistakes. You have nine hundred ninety-nine to go." Just before he said that, my Perfectionist had said, *You idiot! I knew you would blow it. You should have known better.* It is obvious which perspective I prefer, but it's hard to filter out the voice that says I'm an idiot for making a mistake.

My teacher's wisdom was a great help to me. He didn't indulge me by telling me that I hadn't make a mistake; we both knew I had. Yet he knew that I didn't deserve to be shot for it. I wanted such wisdom to live inside of me, so I could call on it to sustain me through challenges. With my teacher's help, the help of many others, and my own determination to accept myself, I did find wisdom. Then I lost it, found it again, lost it, found it again . . . and so it goes.

"Anything but Ordinary!"

A good way to detect the presence of the Perfectionist is to notice how you feel about being human, as opposed to superhuman. Does humanness seem boring and ordinary? Does being merely human feel like a terrible fate? I have known people who would rather be thought of as criminals than as ordinary humans.

At one time, I couldn't bear to be ordinary. I had to think of myself as special, not like anyone else. Yet I hid the qualities that actually made me unique. I was afraid to show my uniqueness because it had not been well-received, afraid that in trying to show something special I'd reveal something weird. So I played it safe and stayed within the norm of acceptable behavior, and inside I felt restless and hollow.

My perfectionist is the part of me that fears I am not special. Even today my self-judgment tells me, every chance it gets, *If you can't be funny and brilliant, have the sense to keep your mouth shut!* This kind of feedback is hardly conducive to relaxed self-expression!

A Master of Disguises

Let us examine some of the many different ways that the Perfectionist can operate. Because these cover a wide span of possibilities, you will see yourself reflected in some, but not all, of them. Use any new information you glean to deepen your awareness of how perfectionism currently inhibits you. Keep reminding yourself that, once your Perfectionist has been properly harnessed, you will get to be the driver rather than the driven.

It is crucial to remember that the Perfectionist often disguises itself as Inner Guidance. It does this through many kinds of trickery, misusing our personal virtues and even universal truths to get us to obey its dictates. Why? Because it is simply too afraid to let life be what it is. The following are just some of the impersonations of which it is capable.

Obsession

When the Perfectionist manifests as obsession, you may be plagued by invasive thoughts. Sometimes the obsessiveness is accompanied by compulsive behavior or a driving urge to act. This urgency combined with aggressive thoughts is the red flag that reveals the Perfectionist.

I have never known Inner Guidance to be bossy; it rests in the truth that needs neither to push nor to persuade. But I have so many times been hounded by my thoughts and coerced by my feelings of urgency that I finally discovered a pattern to these obsessions: need combined with fear. The need is backed by a fear that I can't have whatever it is I need, because it has been forbidden in some way in the past. The need itself may be completely legitimate. But, because it has been blocked, I feel that if I don't speed toward the object of the need and grab it fast, I will lose it.

Obsession can be connected to many things, such as money, power, or love. I will use love as an example. Sometimes obsession is confused with love, and sometimes it coexists with love when there is fear that the love won't be returned. In this case, the openhearted flow of love is replaced by a fearful dread of loss, and the invasive thought says with certainty, *He/she could never love me.* Sometimes an urgent need to secure and possess the other's love is backed by such thoughts as, *I must have this person's love. I am worthless without it. I will never find love again. I will die without it.* These thoughts are so powerful that they seem like absolute truth. But their very thrust gives them away. Inner Guidance does not have velocity behind it, because it is neither afraid nor attached. It is the quiet sage within us, that patiently waits to be noticed . . . at the end of the roller coaster ride.

Inner Guidance comes naturally when one is open to it. There is no need to do anything; you don't even have to think. Thinking makes active use of the mind to seek solutions. With Inner Guidance, the mind only asks and receives. The guidance arrives out of the void, pulled by invitation. Certain attitudes invite Inner Guidance, while others increase the Perfectionist's control. One needs to learn to distinguish these.

My client Carol said she felt guided to send a letter to her boyfriend, who had lately been distant, telling him to never call her again. She didn't want him to think she needed him. She didn't want him to think ill of her, and she planned to restore her image with this letter. Her urgency to control his opinion of her was so great that she could not wait to mail the letter. By morning, she felt quite different, and called to ask him not to open the letter.

Practice has given Carol self-knowledge. She has learned to use these situations to distinguish Inner Guidance from obsession. That urgent desire to communicate an ultimatum was her tip-off. She now knows about her image perfectionism, and knows that if she feels as if she can't wait, the feeling is not coming from Inner Guidance.

If you can sit with your thoughts, impulses, or strong feelings instead of acting them out, you can start to tell where they come from. True guidance can be inspiring, sobering, or something in between, but a feeling of rightness and natural flow always comes with it.

The Trickster

When the Perfectionist takes control, it suppresses our sense of humor and brings out our self-righteousness. This leaves us vulnerable to the most slippery character in the psyche: the Trickster.

The Trickster is the crazy-maker that clouds judgment. It's the way that we unwittingly fool ourselves into thinking the truth is the opposite of what it really is. It creates a false truth, and it can be found at the core of some of our most embarrassing moments. Can you remember times when you felt certain you were totally right about something, only to find out you were totally wrong? A sure sign that the Trickster has been at play! The Trickster is that convincing voice that makes us feel so certain while in the midst of making a big mistake. The importance of the mistake then feels exaggerated, because mistakes—instead of being viewed as natural occurrences—are forbidden. That intense feeling of being in the right should be as much cause for suspicion as a powerful feeling of wrongness. Either is a signal that the Perfectionist (in the form of the Trickster) is at the helm.

Three days past payday, Lois worked up the courage to ask Robert, her boss, for her paycheck. Robert said defensively, "What are you talking about? You got your paycheck." From fear of contradicting her boss, Lois started to panic, but she held her ground, saying, "No, I didn't get my paycheck." Robert went angrily to his checkbook, to prove to Lois that he was right and she was wrong, but he couldn't find the entry because he had forgotten to write the check. He then felt embarrassed, and angry with himself for his mistake. But, because she had discovered him, he defended his error by being cold toward her.

The sting of such events can be greatly diminished, if we allow a margin for error and forgive our own and others' mistakes. Then, such incidents can even serve as comic relief.

Until we recognize the Trickster as an unavoidable fact of life, the screwups that it causes us all to make will evoke shame and humiliation, as well as heated arguments. The task is to wake up to each trick without feeling angry for falling for it in the first place. The Trickster must be approached with a sense of humor. It drives our self-importance into the ground, and teaches humility by making fools of us until we don't mind being fools anymore. To defuse the Trickster helps in defusing the Perfectionist. The challenge is to accept with a light heart that we will trick ourselves when we least expect it, over and over again. We can then volunteer to keep a playful vigil for the Trickster's appearances.

The gift of the Trickster is to teach us to recognize the Perfectionist, so that we can reclaim our sense of humor. After we have made friends with the Trickster, we experience that the growth we seek comes from accepting those parts of ourselves that we once believed to be flawed.

Ambition

Ambition, according to Merriam-Webster, means "The eager desire for success, honor, or power." Ambition is a natural part of the human experience. When it is tempered with awareness and trust (in ourselves and life), we feel encouraged toward our goals. Without awareness and trust, ambition misleads us by becoming blind ambition. When this happens, the Perfectionist is in control. The Perfectionist ignores all factors that are counter to ambition's goal. When it manifests as blind ambition, it recognizes only those factors that further the goal.

The Perfectionist doesn't understand the nature of change. Real change is slow. It begins with recognition and acceptance of the actual, rather than a jump to a preferred starting place. Real change requires continual revisions of the plan. The Perfectionist's blind ambition is so attached to the goal that it rejects all opposing forces, such as the need for more time, support, preparation, or course corrections.

Dorothy's parents were Holocaust survivors. The life they wanted was stolen from them, and many of their dreams and longings were lost forever. It was natural for them to transfer those dreams to Dorothy and her brother. They feared for their daughter and their son, because they well knew the dangers of life. With the best of intentions, they inadvertently instilled a fearful urgency in both of their children.

Dorothy felt guilty for wanting a different life than her parents wanted for her. Her parents' ambition for her was so extreme that they could not see her nature. As my client, Dorothy had to wake up to her brand of perfectionism: the good daughter who must spare her parents another disappointment. She had to build a bridge between loyalty to her nature and loyalty to her parents and heritage.

Idealism

Idealism is a helpful resource because it can see all the possibilities. It can inspire the building of bridges between many different perspectives and opposing forces. It can find that silver lining in the storm cloud and see the good in something seemingly adverse. Idealism only becomes troublesome when it excludes other evidence. If we need to see the good, a defense against seeing the bad is operating.

When idealism is used as a defense, that positive sense of what could be becomes a rigid "should be." Used in this way, idealism is yet another disguise of the Perfectionist—one that insists that all is (or should be) perfect.

Beverly refuses to see anything but goodness and light. She's had a series of relationships with men who abuse her, yet she will not recognize the abuse because she needs to see her world and her men as good. Her eternal optimism protects her against the disappointment and despair she would have to face if she allowed herself to realize that she has spent her life playing the victim. Beverly hasn't integrated her spiritual beliefs with her personal life. While insisting that there are no victims, she endures black eyes and death threats. Her idealism assures her that she will always keep on the sunny side, even as her life is being degraded.

Claudia, unlike Beverly, knows that she plays the victim. But instead of leaving the situations and relationships that do her harm, she dedicates her idealism to the rehabilitation of her victimizers. She is caught in "It should be perfect and I will make it so." Her perfectionistic idealism insists that she will make others see the light.

The Rebel

When the Perfectionist masquerades as the Rebel, it has gotten its wires crossed regarding power. The Rebel first emerges when we are about two years old, and feels its first satisfying power when saying, "No!" A child needs to be allowed to say no to authority figures in order to become his or her own authority. If the parents have the wisdom to allow this minor rebellion, the child soon enough passes through this phase. Then, as a natural part of the growth process, the Rebel emerges again in adolescence to meet the teenager's need to feel strong and unique.

If the parents can recognize this rebelliousness as another necessary phase and handle it moderately, the Rebel will strengthen the emerging adult's identity. But if the parents enter into a power struggle with the Rebel and try to break the rebelliousness, they will unintentionally encourage their child to fuse with the rebel identity. After the young person leaves home, the power struggle will be repeated with other authority figures. Until autonomy is won, the individual will be stuck fighting and saying "No!"—even to his or her own dreams.

Leslie was a painter who fought long and hard against her mother for artistic freedom. Her mother found Leslie's paintings indecent, and tried to stop her from wasting her time shocking people. When Leslie started to receive critical acclaim for her work, her mother changed positions and began to take public credit with a proud "my-daughter-the-artist" stance. This so infuriated Leslie's Rebel that, to get back at her mother, she destroyed all of her paintings. Leslie was a rebel against her own cause.

The Rebel is halfway to freedom, and a necessary part of our psyche, yet it has not learned self-mastery. Rebellion is another form of perfectionism when the Rebel gets caught in a reaction against the Perfectionist and unleashes self-destructive power. The Rebel needs to learn to say yes to life.

Responsibility

Our sense of responsibility in adulthood reflects the relationship we had with our parents. To bridge the extremes of Helpless and the Perfectionist, we need to release responsibility where we have taken too much, so that we can take more responsibility where we have not taken enough. Until we readjust this balance, our relationships as adults will be little more than echoes of our childhood.

Susan feels frustrated that when she expresses her grievances to her husband, Tim, he turns into a child. Yet she unwittingly attacks and ridicules him with such comments as "I have to do everything myself if it's going to be done right" and "You're not even a man." Tim cannot bear any more complaints. His deep sense of failure prevents him from accepting his share of the responsibility. Susan's Perfectionist gets projected outward as self-righteousness. Tim's Perfectionist gets turned inward as self-contempt. Together, they relive their childhood experiences. Susan's mother was helpless in certain areas, so Susan became a perfectionistic parent. Tim had a perfectionistic parent who never taught him self-reliance, so in certain areas he remained a helpless child.

Susan's inability to tolerate the disparity between what she needs and what she receives from Tim is a reflection of her childhood experience. Her child self screams through her anger to be heard, but Susan is the one who can't hear it. Though she rejected certain self-care needs long ago, the needs still wait for her to take responsibility for meeting them. True to her training, she resentfully takes care of Tim instead. Tim, too, replays his childhood—caught in repeated attempts to please Mom through Susan.

Both have taken too much responsibility for each other and not enough for themselves. The challenge is not for them to change themselves or each other, but for both of them to identify and change their relationship to responsibility. Until they separate the past from the present, and bring an adult perspective to their childhood experiences, they will continue to believe that they both need to repair Tim.

Guilt

Guilt is the result of crossed wires regarding self-care, which is how we take responsibility for ourselves, how we say yes to ourselves. The Perfectionist, in its wish to make us strong, good people, believes that our need for self-care is weak and indulgent. It further believes that self-nurturing is not a valid reason to say no to someone else. Guilt, in this sense, is an indicator that there is an internal law against saying no.

When it springs from conscience to prevent or correct a misguided act, guilt is a helpful signal. But the crafty Perfectionist poses as conscience to control us. It uses guilt as an electric fence to jolt us away from the freedom of choice.

Doris's sister Helen asked to borrow money to start a new business with her husband. They had already lost two businesses and defaulted on two loans. Doris did not want to give them the money, because she was fairly sure they would lose it, but her guilt would not let her say no. She lent them the money, but resented it and leaked hostile comments to them and others. Helen got angry about being made the object of Doris's guilt trips, and felt justified when she and her husband could not repay the loan. Doris and Helen have not spoken in five years.

In following the dictates of her guilt, Doris acted against her Inner Guidance. If Doris had been able to withstand her guilt, Helen might have been disappointed and angry, but Doris would still have her money—probably a relationship with her sister, too. It cost her more to say yes than it would have to say no. The highest cost of all is the anger she now holds against herself for not trusting her own instincts, which is the Perfectionist punishing her for following the Perfectionist. When one obeys guilt, there is no freedom to give, because there is no freedom to not give. A guilt-generated gift has consequences, such as deprivation or resentment for the giver and the guilt trip that is imposed upon the receiver.

We can't simply wait and expect guilt to go away, for it's too deeply ingrained. We have to learn how to live with guilt and weather its storms, without letting it take control. Instead of believing the guilt, we can bear its discomfort long enough to ask Inner Guidance to deliver a more profound imperative than the wish to avoid guilt. Following Inner Guidance can relieve self-blame by giving us a wiser perspective, and thereby changing our relationship to guilt.

When we refuse to follow guilt, we can expect at first to feel even more guilt. We will probably feel that bothersome knot in the stomach that accompanies any transgression of the Perfectionist's laws. But, even if breaking it makes us feel like an outlaw, this is a law that needs to be broken.

So that you may see perfectionism in action in its various guises, this book will illustrate many of the Perfectionist's antics—through my own story and, later, through the stories of some of my clients. But first we will explore the nine major types of perfectionism that I have encountered.

4

Nine Kinds
of Perfectionism

E very variety of perfectionism represents an attempt to maintain control. Since different types of injury give rise to different types of perfectionism, each variety seeks a different kind of control. Yet all are based on an underlying fear that the injury will be repeated; the control is an attempt to avoid the anticipated reinjury. And each variety (specific area of injury) of perfectionism, when it holds sway over the personality, is cut off from Essence, cut off from reality, and cut off from contact with the outside world.

I believe that we all have at least three of the following nine types of perfectionism* to some degree, with one type predominating. Although they are compartmentalized in their listing here, they actually overlap and blend together in the personality, creating a unique form of perfectionism in each one of us.

I include possible childhood origins for these types of perfectionism—what may have happened in the early family life—only to convey the dynamics that create the different types. I have no wish to criticize parents. The challenge of raising a family is so immense that perfect parenting is impossible. All of us will leave an imprint on our children.

---

* These delineations of types of perfectionism reflect the author's point of view. They are derived from the study of the Michael teachings, as set down by Chelsea Quinn Yarbro, and the Enneagram personality types. In those systems, they are identified as chief features and addictions, and are not directly linked to perfectionism.

With hindsight, many of us would have done certain things differently. But only the Perfectionist could expect us to have known what we had not yet learned.

Arrogance: The Fear of Being Vulnerable

Afflicted with a strong belief that it has something to hide that is defective or otherwise unacceptable, Arrogance covers its fear with a facade of invulnerability. It seeks to hold itself together and to never reveal weakness—not even to itself. This type of perfectionism pours a lot of energy into keeping up the appearance of high self-esteem.

Arrogance attempts to compensate for its imagined deficiency by countering the "I'm afraid I'm defective" belief with behaviors that say, "I'm better, stronger, wiser, tougher, and smarter." The fear of being exposed is countered by aloofness; the need for acceptance, by detachment. Arrogance can be boastful to cover insecurity, can be loud to cover extreme shyness, or can take pride in its humility.

The arrogant perfectionist often finds ways to demonstrate that perfection already exists, and may be completely unaware of using countermeasures. Individuals caught up in Arrogance may simply think of themselves as confident and superior. They may feel that they either don't or shouldn't have limitations, and behave accordingly. They often explain the absence of deep relationships in their lives by taking the stance that they haven't found anyone good enough, strong enough, smart enough, loving enough, and so forth.

Arrogance is my primary form of perfectionism. Those of us who are afflicted by Arrogance want to be seen and accepted for who we are, but our arrogance ensures that this will never happen. We miss opportunities for intimacy because others respond or react to our facade, and not to the real person underneath. We are treated insensitively because Arrogance doesn't show its sensitivity, often wearing a poker face instead. Arrogance can be so unwelcoming and unapproachable that people stay away.

Arrogance often protects itself from being rejected by rejecting first, or at least feigning disinterest. There is a secret romantic wish for someone to see through the mask and spare these individuals the dreaded self-exposure. This, of course, does not happen, which increases the loneliness and deprivation that arise from maintaining the facade.

Arrogance operates on the belief that the person it covers is unacceptable, until this becomes a self-fulfilling prophecy.

Arrogance in Childhood

As children, these individuals often felt alien in their own family, school, and community. They were not allowed or supported to appreciate their differences. Instead, they felt a constant sense of exposure and vulnerability. They may have felt criticized or attacked, and that they had no way to stop the assault other than by pretending not to be affected. They feared that if they felt or showed their real emotions they would be overcome by them, or would once again be regarded as strange. Their pervasive need for protection created an armored or detached persona.

When I was in high school, a friend who could see beneath my cover called me Sweet Cindy, which made me cringe and want to cover her mouth. I saw sweetness as weakness. I wanted to be thought of as cool and tough—certainly not sweet, which could make me a target for further harm.

Self-Deprecation: The Fear of Being Inferior

Self-Deprecation dreads inadequacy. It fears not being good enough, not living up to expectations. Of all the nine types, it has the most visible shyness and low self-esteem, although it is actually not as shy as Arrogance. In this type, perfectionism arose as a constant striving to be good enough, not just in appearance but in substance. Self-Deprecation is often underestimated by others because it so clearly underestimates itself. It responds to opportunities with, "Who, me?"

People stuck in Self-Deprecation fail to see the virtues that they possess, admiring these attributes in other people but not recognizing them in themselves. They have insufficient pride in their own positive qualities to balance their self-abasement. Because Self-Deprecation disregards and underestimates itself, it also tends to be slighted by others.

In disagreements, Self-Deprecation is quick to defer to others: "You're probably right. I'm probably wrong." It doesn't trust its own convictions. Self-Deprecation's body often looks uncomfortable. Even the most graceful have a slightly apologetic posture, or downcast eyes. At a social gathering, these individuals prefer to have a job to do. They will offer to cook or clean up at the party. Self-Deprecation is the wallflower that craves to be noticed, yet finds attention painful when it is received. It's the good girl and good boy, very concerned about falling out of favor.

Often, when people in Self-Deprecation attempt to increase their sense of self-worth, they adopt characteristics of Arrogance. And when people in Arrogance attempt to decrease their self-inflation, they adopt characteristics of Self-Deprecation. Both of these measures represent an attempt to assume the form until the essence can be achieved.

In relationships, people in Self-Deprecation may bond too quickly out of gratitude for being chosen, without discerning whether the other is someone they would choose. Their obvious need for approval frequently causes them to be dismissed or ridiculed by other people (e.g., Sally Field's statement at the Academy awards: "You really like me!").

Self-Deprecation in Childhood

As children, these individuals were caused to feel that they didn't live up to what was expected of them. Their virtues were not sufficiently mirrored. Instead of being praised for an achievement, they found that what they hadn't accomplished was noticed. If they got an A minus, it should have been an A. If they had made the team, they hadn't yet won any games. This may have been a parent's attempt to motivate, but it actually demoralized the child.

Sometimes they were praised, but not for the personal qualities that they valued. For example, perhaps Susan wanted to be appreciated for her intelligence, but her father would only tell her how pretty she was.

Image Vanity: A Poor Body Image

Image Vanity regarding the body or persona is an intense form of self-disparagement. Like Self-Deprecation, it fears being perceived as not good enough, but it has a different focus and solution. Image Vanity's compensation for the fear is a fixation on appearance. Having the right look or act replaces substance. The image perfectionist thinks, *What impression do I want to make? Who should I be to win them over?* There is a hollowness to the personality. The behavior seems sincere, but others can't "feel" these individuals. They are often regarded as phony or superficial.

Image perfectionists imagine that others are always thinking about them, and thinking the same things they think about themselves. They try to work on themselves, responding to the real or imagined opinions of others. But it is really their own perfectionistic opinions that cause their problems. When our Perfectionist believes that we are unacceptable, we think that the whole world believes it, as well.

Image Vanity perfectionism can cause the same insecurity and suffering in a near-perfect body as it can in an obese one. It fixates on body image through clothes, exercise, eating disorders, the latest diet, cosmetic surgery, and so on. Too much time and energy go into trying to control and perfect the body, or into thinking about trying to control and perfect the body.

Often there is a feeling of contempt for the body, as if the body has failed the individual, and an overidentification with the physical form (*I am my body*). Regardless of whether the body is fat, thin, or in good proportion, it is not good enough for the person trapped in Image Vanity. This form of perfectionism creates an attitude distortion that says, *If my body is not perfect, I am unlovable.*

Sometimes there is a perceptual distortion, as when the anorexic looks into the mirror and sees fat even when she is dangerously underweight. In the case of overeaters, there is an emotional craving that they attempt to satisfy with food. Food is the substitute comfort for what is really craved: the experience of taking nourishment from Essence.

In our society, we are constantly besieged by advertisements that link perfect bodies with the culture's notions of success. These serve as false confirmation to Image Vanity that it is on the right track. The obsession with the body can be so great that it obscures a person's ability to reach for worthier goals. Opportunities are missed because the person thinks, *When I get thin/increase my chest measurement/change my nose, then I'll be happy, motivated, deserving, and successful.* Chances to find fulfillment may be right before these individuals' eyes, but they can't see them because they remain fixated on the making of preliminary repairs.

In this kind of perfectionism, self-deceit, inflation, deflation, and promotion go hand-in-hand. Margaret Frings Keyes, author of *The Enneagram Relationship Workbook*, has put it well: "Whenever our self-image is fundamental to our self-esteem, there is a temptation to enhance it at the cost of truth." It is hard to wake up from inside the image perfectionist's belief system. It takes repeated rounds of failure to inspire a deeper inquiry—an inquiry into Essence, which can give the necessary attitude for lasting change.

Image Vanity in Childhood

As children, these individuals were judged by their appearance or by what people thought of them. Their parents may have modeled image perfectionism as the ideal behavior. In some cases the child witnessed one parent habitually criticizing the other for not looking good enough. A perfect body or image was linked to being lovable, which set the standard by which they received the most love. Sometimes the child was asked to keep secrets in the interest of maintaining appearances. The message was: How it appears is more important than how it is, and how you look is more important than who you are.

Stubbornness: The Fear of Change

In life, change is a constant. Hard as we may try, we cannot control it. Often we can't make the changes we want and can't stop the changes we don't want. To Stubbornness, this is a continual threat. Stubbornness responds to challenges with willful and dogmatic rationales that justify holding to the present course. In those individuals afflicted with this type of perfectionism, the commitment to life goals and the ability to see the big picture are obscured by attachment to a familiar comfort zone.

Stubbornness avoids the new situations it fears by putting more effort into what it has, wants, has decided, has expected, and so on. It is closed to new perspectives. It refuses to keep an open mind because to change its way of thinking could allow for further frightening change. Because it believes that change and flexibility lead to disaster, it may take pride in its determination when actually it is only being obstinate.

When the flow of life is running counter to its own wishes, purposes, or direction, Stubbornness can't acknowledge what is happening. Yet to go against the flow of life as it characteristically does is to incur unnecessary suffering. This suffering could provide an indicator that there is a need to reassess and to consider course corrections, but Stubbornness has too high a tolerance for suffering. Its skin is thick from all the years of protecting itself against the threat of uncontrollable change.

Stubbornness manifests itself in the reluctance to take a healthy risk like leaving a dead-end job or going to a doctor when sick, which results in limited self-growth. Concerned others feel frustrated and shut out, and may try to push Stubbornness in an attempt to be included. But Stubbornness will push back or turn a deaf ear, which causes others to withdraw and eventually to detach from the person. Stubbornness wears blinders to keep its attention on its chosen path and avoid interference. It rejects all the data that is counter to its objectives by thinking, *If I just try harder and use more determination, I'll get the results I want.*

Stubbornness in Childhood

As children, these individuals were not adequately prepared to undergo changes in their lives, because they were somehow placed in unfamiliar and therefore frightening positions with insufficient support. Some form of upheaval caused them to cling to the familiar for safety, and a power struggle may have ensued when a parent tried to force the issue.

Martyrdom: The Fear of Unworthiness

Martyrdom hides its fear of unworthiness by creating a cause for which it can sacrifice itself. It can appear as a smothering mother, a weary volunteer, or the guru who usurps the autonomy of devotees. It utilizes selflessness to feel worthy, and creates a prideful self-esteem from self-sacrifice. This form of perfectionism arises from the need to do good or feel needed to bolster a deficient sense of self-worth.

The entire identity of a person afflicted with Martyrdom can revolve around being important and indispensable to other people. Happiness is dependent, then, on how much control, appreciation, and gratitude is being received for all the care being given. The addiction to martyrdom exists to fill the craving for love that arises from the individual's forgotten personal needs. The truth—that the internal self is bankrupt—is missed in the compulsion to be worthy.

Martyrdom exhausts itself for its cause or for the needs of others. It feels as if it is never doing enough, even as it works itself to death—or wears itself out giving the appearance of working itself to death. Not all martyrs actually do good for others. They may preoccupy themselves with merely thinking about their cause or worrying about the needs of others, or with giving unwanted advice.

To avoid taking responsibility for their own lives, martyrs take too much responsibility for the lives of others. They deem their own lives to be less valuable. There is an unrealistic sense of limitations: *I can bear the weight of the world.* These individuals become a magnet for people who need help, but their efforts to help are not yet grounded in their essence and therefore are frequently not helpful.

For martyrs, relationships with others are like projects. People living in martyrdom cannot have mutual relationships because they cannot acknowledge their own needs, yet there is frequently a hidden IOU in their gifts. The result is a continual loop of perfectionistic helping followed by deprivation, depletion, resentment, loneliness, and, often, somatic illness.

Martyrdom in Childhood

As children, these individuals were caused to feel that they were not sufficiently deserving of whatever they needed. They were required to defer to the needs of other family members, frequently their parents, and were then rewarded in some way for their sacrifice.

When they couldn't get the love they needed for being who they were, they were tempted to try to get it by sweetening the deal: *If you don't love me enough to take care of me, maybe you'll love me more if I take care of you.* They got locked into the perfectionistic pattern of needing to do something special or something more to keep the love coming back to them.

The parents of martyrs may have been martyrs themselves, and may have modeled that as ideal behavior. They may have been unable to parent because they were tired from raising other children. Some of them were children themselves who required their child to assume the parental role. One way or another, they unwittingly transferred to these children an exaggerated sense of responsibility which combined with a feeling of unworthiness to create their Martyrdom complex.

Impatience: The Fear of Missing Something

Impatience arises from the fear of missing out on something important. Those individuals afflicted with this form of perfectionism are trapped in the state of avoiding disappointment. They remember all their past disappointments and use tyranny and intolerance to ensure that they will never be disappointed again.

Perfectionistic impatience has some injury having to do with time. It has to make up for lost time and past disappointments. It creates a pervasive urgency to hurry and get there that only confirms that something important is indeed being missed . . . which causes another disappointment. Its tail-chasing preoccupation with there and then causes it to negate the value of here and now.

Impatience lives in the future, regrets the past, and loses the moment—or chokes it by trying to overstuff it. All its choices are made in the moment. Choices of omission are choices, too; enough of them strung together result in a discrepancy between our self-concept and our behavior: *I have such big plans for myself. I don't know why they're not happening.* Impatience needs to notice that the choices it makes and the actions it takes in each moment do not take it closer to its goals.

Sometimes Impatience has trouble starting something, because the beginning of anything seems like a step backward. There is self-recrimination that says: *I should be further ahead than I am, so I can't slow down. I must speed up.* Impatience feels that it can't take the first step, and may also have trouble completing a given project because it thinks it should already be done. There is no time to finish because it needs to move ahead. It is frequently reluctant to make commitments because something better may come along and it needs to keep its options open.

People caught in Impatience frequently have racing minds. Their thoughts may move so fast that they can't catch them to adequately express themselves. They may speak very fast, or speak in a kind of shorthand by not completing sentences or expressing full thoughts. Anger and frustration are common when they are not understood as quickly as they wish to be. Sometimes they have a short attention span because they are not fully present; their mind wanders to what they are missing.

Impatience sometimes interrupts other people and finishes their sentences for them. A former boss of mine was so impatient that I honed my skill at economy of speech when I talked to him. I tried to say the most I could with the fewest words, because I knew I would lose his attention if I didn't capture it within a few phrases.

Remember, perfectionism arises in specific areas of injury. Joe has Impatience perfectionism, yet he has infinite patience when dealing with inanimate objects such as puzzles, computers, and machines. His impatience arises with other people when he doesn't achieve the objective he wants within his time frame.

Impatience in Childhood

As children, these individuals were not given enough time by their caregivers. They may not have been allowed to learn to express themselves at their own pace, or their participation in events or family discussions was restricted in some way. Perhaps there were too many children in the family, or other priorities diverted the parents' attention.

It is possible that the children were gratified too quickly, instead of being shown the difference between their wants and their needs. Or perhaps the parents themselves were so impatient that the children got the impression they must hurry up to express themselves, or must learn new things at a very fast rate.

Righteousness: The Fear of Being Wrong

Driven by a fear of being wrong, Righteousness strives to be right, to be above reproach, to be perfect and live in a perfect world. It sees life in black and white, with no shades of gray. When Righteousness cannot correct the inner wrongs it perceives, then it projects them onto the outside world. The person stuck in Righteousness becomes a self-appointed reformer with a mission to turn wrong into right. The more zealous the efforts to improve other people's behavior, the more weak the grasp of personal contradictions: *If I can't fix me, let me double my efforts to fix you instead.*

Righteousness gets caught in a vicious circle in which rumination and deliberation replace decision and purposeful action, due to a morbid fear of making a mistake. Mistakes are viewed as sins, deserving of severe punishment. The unconscious thought is: *I will feel better if I look at your behavior and decisions than if I look at my own.*

Because mistakes are sins, there may be a preoccupation with order that stifles the life out of the creative process and the pleasure out of human relationships. Sometimes there is an abhorrence of clutter, uncleanliness, or loose ends. Righteousness pays too much attention to the actions of others. There is an intolerance of people who do not correctly meet the standards.

As with other types of perfectionism, not everyone in Righteousness will exhibit all of the listed characteristics. Perfectionism shows itself in specific areas of injury, so a person trapped in Righteousness may be fine with a messy house but unable to abide a person not returning their phone call—not because they feel personally slighted, mind you, but because such a lapse is incorrect.

Order is elevated to the status of a high virtue because it requires action, which reduces anxiety by conveying a feeling of things getting done. The maintaining of order also promises a perfect result, and allows the person afflicted with Righteousness to avoid those more purposeful actions that could result in a mistake. Unfortunately, the obsession with order creates a concomitant lack of appreciation for the learning experience.

Righteousness gives off a seething resentment, because life is not as it should be. When this form of perfectionism holds sway, the face has a stern, serious, and holier-than-thou appearance. Those in the presence of a person caught in Righteousness feel intimidated and judged as inadequate. They may react with insecurity or may rebel and refuse to rise to the standards set before them. The burden on the shoulders of Righteousness is impossibly heavy and wearing. Even if life becomes easier and certain goals are achieved, this brings little pleasure, for new goals become loftier so as to stay just out of reach.

Fulfillment is a threat to Righteousness because anger and dissatisfaction are at the core of its drive. This is an addiction that cannot be released for fear that no other motivating force for perfection exists. If Righteousness discovers that perfection already exists, in the human rather than superhuman sense, it suffers a loss of purpose and meaning in life. But this is the very threshold that must be crossed, if Righteousness is to overcome its bitter, cynical loneliness.

Righteousness in Childhood

As children, these individuals were premature adults with a harsh internal voice of authority. They either identified with and emulated a righteous parent, or found it necessary to take on the parental role themselves to fill a lack in the parenting they received. They lived in a fault-finding environment, where blame and criticism between family members replaced mutual acceptance and respect. Eventually their anger obscured their essence, and became the motivating force prompting them to right wrongs and create the perfection they seek.

Greed-Envy: The Fear of Lack

Greed-Envy springs from the fear that there will be a shortage of whatever is needed. There is a perpetual craving because, even if the needs are met, a persistent dread anticipates that all will be lost. Greed-Envy lives in the memory of past losses to reinforce the fear that another loss is coming. It believes that the fulfillment of many of its most critical needs must come from others.

Greed-Envy has a bottomless-pit quality to it, causing others to feel overwhelmed by its intensity. Greed alone is much cooler and more detached, causing others to perceive it as remote and indifferent. Greed-Envy is more hopeful. In both cases, there is a pervasive sense of scarcity. Each type has chosen a different way to remedy the scarcity, and neither challenges the underlying fear. They believe in lack, and adapt accordingly.

Greed needs to realize that it has become impenetrable to fulfillment, while Greed-Envy needs to address the sense of emptiness and mistrust that limits its ability to feel fulfilled. If the desired love, truth, energy, or resources presented themselves, Greed would fail to notice the opportunity and perceive a burden instead. To Greed-Envy, the same opportunity would seem like a drop in the bucket. Both see a false reality in which they have come to believe, and neither see the possibilities that still exist.

In Greed without Envy, there is a belief that what is needed doesn't even exist, which detaches Greed from the wish to fulfill the need. Greed withdraws, withholding its participation in the world by being stingy and miserly to preserve what little is left. It has no faith that more is coming.

Greed-Envy is centered around a specific injury that gave lasting doubt about a need: *I won't have enough truth, knowledge, love, success, freedom, security, energy, time.* This is a different time injury than that of Impatience. Greed wants to hoard time, and Impatience would consider such hoarding to be wasteful of time.

When Greed attaches to Envy there is a competitive voraciousness, causing the person to reach aggressively for whatever is needed. Greed-Envy looks at the world through "have-not" eyes, standing out in the cold with nose pressed against the window of the "haves" and plotting to get in and get more. Greed-Envy causes a person to relentlessly probe, scheme, possess, consume, and interrogate, with an intensity sufficient to push away the very thing that is needed.

The scholar (Greed-Envy for knowledge) fails to recognize when the research is complete; she can't stop gathering data to ever finish writing the book. The husband (Greed-Envy for love) fears his wife won't remain faithful, and badgers her with doubts and questions until he drives her away. The Olympic athlete (Greed-Envy to win), unable to trust that honest efforts lead to success, undermines a competitor and destroys her own career.

Greed-Envy in Childhood

As children, these individuals felt deprived of personal contact or the kind of love and attention they needed. In an attempt to compensate for the deprivation, they learned to derive comfort from fixating on substitutes.

Greed-Envy fixated on truth is my secondary form of perfectionism. I flip back and forth from Greed-Envy to just Greed. The Envy emerged from watching my younger brother get the love that was withheld from me. The Greed-Envy came out of my need to confirm the truth of my perceptions, which I was continually told were dreams, lies, or my imagination. I needed others to agree with me before I could believe myself. So I set about to prove my truth to others, as a compensation for my fragile self-trust.

Self-Destruction: The Fear of Losing Control

Self-Destruction fears a loss of control that will lead to a breakdown. It harms itself in an attempt to prevent an anticipated greater harm. Its misguided survival mechanism goes into overdrive to stay ahead of impending collapse. Self-Destruction overrides self-care needs—often to the point of danger.

Individuals who have eating disorders are subject to perfectionism in the form of Self-Destruction. Anorexia and bulimia are extreme attempts to stay in control; each can result in hospitalization and death. A person in Self-Destruction may take caffeine or amphetamines to wake up, alcohol to relax, and barbiturates to go to sleep—all methods that work in the short run but are damaging over time.

Self-Destruction is terrified that something bad will happen if control is given up. But it is the refusal to relinquish control that causes bad things to happen. For example, artists who fear losing control of their creative flow may work themselves to exhaustion: *If I stop, I may lose my muse and never start again.* They ignore their body signals to rest or eat, or they use those signals as reminders to punch up their energy so they can keep going. Unable to trust life's process of ebb and flow, they find ways to work the angles, to keep control of their artistry. This can result in Self-Destruction disguised as the virtue "Starving for Art." Those who are trapped in Self-Destruction are in danger of tearing themselves down too far in their attempt to rebuild themselves into a better, more idealized form.

Self-Destruction in Childhood

As children, these individuals may have suffered a specific trauma, such as a prolonged illness or a severe physical or emotional injury, that left an impression of having no control. Perhaps there were unpredictable episodes of abuse or neglect that caused them to feel as if they were being destroyed and were powerless to save themselves.

To compensate for their sense of impending crisis, they learned ways to simulate a feeling of being in control, but the forms of control that they chose caused the very destruction that they wished to avoid. If the parents were also in Self-Destruction, these children never learned how to self-care. As they matured, they failed to recognize the consequences of their form of control. For instance, smoking is known to cause cancer, but Self-Destruction says, *It won't happen to me.*

Self-Destruction is the third form of perfectionism that emerged from my specific injury. The three forms work together. My inflated Arrogance says, *I'm tough. I have no limits,* while my deflated Arrogance says, *I'm defective and have to try harder.* My Greed-Envy says, *I have to know "the truth," as others do,* and my Self-Destruction adds, *. . . so I can avoid the breakdown that is surely coming.* In actuality, when my forms of perfectionism are engaged I am vulnerable, I don't trust my truth, and I wear myself out, sometimes to the point of breakdown.

To remain in control of myself and so meet my Perfectionist's demands, I ignored my self-care needs and pushed my limits until I contracted Chronic Fatigue Immune Dysfunction Syndrome (CFIDS). This is a chronic flu-like state, usually initially triggered by some kind of trauma. Once an individual has CFIDS, it flares up whenever balance is lost. The return to good health requires acceptance, patience, flexibility, and committed self-care.

This consequence of my perfectionism has repeatedly brought me to my knees, yet I consider my CFIDS to be a blessing as well as a curse. For it is this chronic condition that led to my change of perspective and deeper inquiry into Essence.

5

My Life as a
Good Girl/Bad Girl

I have never seen a picture of my grandparents, and as a child I didn't know their names. My mother, Ruth, was the unwanted only child of two alcoholics. Her bedroom was a cot beneath the clothes hanging in the closet. Her father's favorite method of discipline was to dangle her by her feet from the window of their third-story apartment. While swinging her over the street below and threatening to drop her, he laughed at her terror. She and her mother, in constant fear of his contempt and violence, maintained a cowed silence when he was at home. Her mother died at forty-two, during the delirium tremens that accompany alcohol withdrawal. My mother never told me how the loss affected her, or anything else about my grandmother.

The first time my mother dared to talk back to her father, she then ran away from home, certain that he would kill her if she stayed. He had ordered her to return to the store for an item he'd forgotten to put on the list. She bowed and said, "Yes, God." He moved toward her, asking, "What did you say?" She repeated, "Yes, God . . . damn you!" and ran to the bathroom, where she climbed out the window, walked a ledge, and fled through the apartment next door. She was sixteen.

Mom never got to be a child, never felt safe for a moment. For the next ten years, she struggled to take care of herself, working in theaters at night so she could attend school during the day. She sewed her own clothes. During World War II, she worked in the shipyards.

A Black Cloud

Life, for my mother, was always a struggle for survival. She hoped that marrying my father would change some of that. He was a charmer, and they had fun times dancing together in nightclub shows. It seemed, for a time, that life might get easier for her. Too soon, however, my mother became pregnant with me, which cast a black cloud over my parents' marriage. As Mom later told me, my birth was an intrusion in their life.

My father continued to see other women after he married Mom. Following my birth, when my mother was twenty-six, he started staying out all night and his girlfriends began calling the house. Answering the phone, Mom would become unhinged when, instead of hanging up, the other women treated her as if she were Dad's secretary. Her nerves were shot, and she couldn't eat. In a photo of her holding me shortly after my birth, she has none of the vibrancy of her earlier snapshots. Her hands look skeletal, and her eyes are vacant.

My mother's stories about my birth had nothing to do with me. There was no mention of the traditional joy that surrounds a new addition to the family. My birth was her nightmare, although the labor was easy: I came so fast, she almost had me in the elevator. My very existence was the problem. I was too much for her, too soon. She admittedly resented my presence, feeling that I had made life more difficult for her and had cost her her marriage. "You owe me," she often reminded me. "I brought you into this world."

My Mother's Self-Hate

My father left when I was about six months old. According to my mother, she gave him the money to leave and kept his debts, just to be rid of him. He went on to have another family that he later abandoned as well. Mom worked two jobs to support the two of us, and was seldom home. She tells me I had a series of crazy, drunken baby-sitters. She once came home to find me crawling under the ironing board, my sitter passed out on top of it and a hot iron dangling over the side.

Mom was given to frequent violent rages. She blamed my birth, my drunken baby-sitters, and my "rotten s.o.b." father as the cause of them. Mom also blamed my paternal grandmother, often insisting, "She talked me into marrying your father. I should never have done it. I could shoot myself for listening to her."

Mom says I made her yell at me—that I upset her whenever I talked. From as early as I can remember, this was an ongoing theme. My mother needed silence during meals and when she was reading. I was also forbidden to speak when the news was on TV, but I kept forgetting and was continually startled by her reaction. She'd scream, "Shut up!" when the first syllable was out of my mouth, beyond retrieval. "I told you, I told you, not to talk when I'm watching the news! Why do you that?" she would yell. When I tried to answer her, she'd slap my face and shout, "Don't talk back!" She beat me with her hands or a belt, starting when I was five. The walls were marked from the times I ran from her and the belt hit the wall instead. Eventually, I began to jump and yelp when she merely entered the room, a startle reflex that continues today.

I watched, half terrified and half amazed, as she seemed to take cues from an internal voice and work herself into a rage. She would grab my hair and pull me around the house, screaming, "You liar! You're evil, evil! You're going to grow up to be a nothing. You'll be a slut who lives off men, a slut!" Even in normal conversation, Mom repeated herself often, trying to be heard. It took me many years to realize that she was talking to herself. Mom hated herself, and was trying to prevent me from becoming like her. Later in her life, she told me that inside her head was a constant, deafening roar.

When she wasn't angry, Mom was in bed, reading or sleeping to recover from overwork and depression. I was either in trouble or didn't exist. Her rages were unpredictable, and no matter what I did or didn't do, I couldn't stop them. I seemed unable to stay out of her way. I think I preferred her violence to her neglect. I needed the contact.

Mom has told me that we never bonded because she was always working, always exhausted, and had nothing to give me emotionally— she couldn't kiss or touch. She's said that she felt especially guilty about the time I asked her to kiss me before she went to work. She said, "I'm late." I said, "There's always time for love." My comment struck her like a blow, but she still couldn't bring herself to kiss me.

The Refuge of Perfectionism

I began to grow into a perfectionist right from the start. I was so desperate for love and attention that I put on a perpetual performance to get it. Hearing my mother brag that I could use big words at the age of three was my cue to astonish all with my brilliance, in order to garner the attention I needed. At four, I told a lady who was hassling a bus driver that she was being exasperating. The whole bus laughed, and gave me a big taste of what I thought I needed. I continued to draw on my talent for knowing what made people like me.

Mom loved movies, and took me to lots of them throughout my childhood. Starting when I was four or five, I would later reenact scenes, hoping to win her attention. When I couldn't get any sign from her that she approved of my performances, I spied on her conversations to hear her tell others about them.

Even in the midst of her bitterness, Mom had a terrific sense of humor, and I loved it when she laughed. One of my favorite memories is of her enjoying the *I love Lucy* show. I would laugh as she laughed. She also had a courageous, warrior-like spirit in a crisis—something she passed on to me. One morning in Golden Gate Park, I remember that a man jumped out of the bushes, naked under a trench coat, and exposed himself to us. Instead of freaking out and running away, Mom ran toward him, feigning enthusiasm. He ran away from us. With a deadpan delivery, she said, "That gets them every time." I was in awe, because the mother I knew lived on a panic button. Watching her treat this like a nonevent was the beginning of a series of lessons in how to be strong in the world.

I often felt a frantic striving inside of me, a continual sense of urgency to fill a need that I could not name. Caught in the infinity loop of trying harder and harder, while falling farther and farther away from what I most needed, I was certain there was something terribly wrong with me. Fortunately, I had someone loving to turn to who made me feel special.

Mom Versus Grandma

My paternal grandmother was the love of my life. In her house, my world was perfect. *I* was perfect. Grandma adored me, and showered me with gifts and attention. Together we sang just the happy parts of different songs: "Travelin' along, singin' a song, side by side . . ." Her enormous bosom was my pillow; I buried my face there with complete abandon and no trace of the self-consciousness that pervaded my other life.

Mom saw conspiracies everywhere. She swore that Grandma didn't really love me, that she spoiled me to make her look bad. But I went to

Grandma's house as often as I could. Grandma made me chocolate pudding, and we saved change in a big jar for our dream vacation to Disneyland. She gave me a stuffed Airedale that I named Mikey, after the dog I saw with her in her old photos. Times with Grandma were a heavenly escape from the hell at home.

Bob entered our lives when I was four or five, and Mom soon married him. In the beginning he was kind to us, helping my mother take care of me. He would dress me for school and brush my hair, and I loved the gentleness of his touch. One night, through my sleep, I felt him in bed with me. The initial impression has stayed with me my whole life. It was an ideal experience of warm body contact in the night, one I would search for again and again. Then the world went sideways. I didn't know what was happening, but I froze in silent fear.

Later I told Grandma, "Bob peed on me." She urged me to tell my mother, but when I did, Grandma was blamed for poisoning me against her, for trying to ruin Mom's life. I heard Mom tell Grandma that she couldn't see me anymore without supervision. Grandma said, "If I can't see her alone, I'll never see her again." She turned, her head held high, walked past me in the foyer without a glance, and went out the door and out of my life forever. My only support figure was gone by the time I was six, and it was all my fault.

Daydreams and Nightmares

I don't remember having a single feeling about it, or mentioning Grandma ever again. Now I know that I shattered into a million pieces. Regarding my accusations, Bob and Mom took me to a therapist, and they all told me I'd had a bad dream. I retreated from the outer world into a rich inner world of fantasy. I can remember very little of my life between the ages of six and nine, though I vividly recall my daydreams and recurrent nightmares.

In one nightmare I was afraid, and sneaking into bed with Mom even though Bob was on the other side of her. Certain that I was awake, I watched a trap door lower from the ceiling and a monster advance toward me in slow motion. I would look at my mother and think, *This can't be happening! I'm awake, Mom is right here—how can he still be coming to get me?* Then I would feel the world go sideways again. I began to have what I now realize were out-of-body experiences.

When I was nine, my brother was born. My life became vivid again the day he was brought home from the hospital. Mom and Bob beamed with pure happiness at the sight of their baby, and on that day I realized all the love I had missed. I both loved and envied my baby brother, whom they named Darrell. My mother had told me that a hospital nurse named me Cynthia; otherwise I would have had Baby for a first name on my birth certificate. I brooded on how she had proudly named my brother, yet hadn't bothered to come up with a name for me.

Now depression overwhelmed my urgency for attention. I mostly hid in my room, though I still had occasional bursts of striving to get my basic needs met, like going to the neighbors' house with a fantastic story of why I needed them to feed me. There was plenty of food at my house, just no attention. Attention was something I had to make myself worthy of, so I embellished everything, embroidering all my stories to make them more interesting. I built an ideal persona on top of my shattered self, which took a lot of energy and created a falseness about me. I became a representation of the person I thought I should be in the world. Inside, my fantasy self was so special that no one deserved to know me. Peers saw me as confident, aloof, and indifferent to them, but I was actually terrified and felt unworthy of the air I breathed.

Bob owned a bar in the Tenderloin district of San Francisco, and Mom followed in her parents' footsteps by becoming an alcoholic. When I was little, the bar fascinated me. Bob took me to bartending school with him when I was nine. In the bar, I was allowed to mix drinks and wash glasses. As I got older, I was made to stay in the car parked on the street. Before she went into the bar, Mom would deliver a tirade about what would happen to me if I disobeyed her: "Never open this door to anyone but me! These people are crazy around here, crazy! If you open this door before I get out, I'll beat you to a pulp. That is, if you haven't already been brutally murdered. Do you hear me? Do you hear me?"

I waited in the car until two or three in the morning, afraid to sleep because the streets were filled with drug addicts and prostitutes. They knocked on the window and hollered words and phrases I didn't understand. According to my mother, there were also "crazies and murderers" out there. I sat stock still for endless periods, feeling caged, wishing to be invisible to the passersby. Even today, waiting is very difficult for me, for it takes me back to my experiences inside that car.

The Good Daughter

Bob beat Mom, and then Mom beat me. One day, to stop her from battering me because I was refusing to stay home alone with him, I reminded her, "He still does those things to me." Finally, my mother believed me. We moved away from him that day, but now she called me "traitor" and "Lolita." Mom told me I had ruined her life by seducing her husband.

Still hoping to avoid my mother's violence and win her love, I pushed myself to be the kind of daughter I thought she wanted. I learned that, when I behaved as if I were her mother, she acted like a sweet little girl. She would coo in appreciation when I did something nice for her. When I was nine, I spent the money I had saved for Barbie-doll furniture on a birthday gift for Mom: a wrought-iron nightstand to enhance her cherished bedtime experience. I was so proud of myself, dragging it home from the store. When I presented the gift, she looked at me as if I were an angel. I had found the way to my mother's heart. All I had to do was take care of her.

When Mom got angry with me for failing to make her life better, I would get angry with myself. She'd say bitterly, "I work like a dog for you. I've been nice to people all goddamn day." I tried to be good, tried to enjoy taking care of her. But I often hated it—and her for making me do it. I loved the thrill of breaking all of her rules and getting away with it. I became split in two. The exterior me was funny, compliant, and hooked on approval; the inner me was absorbed in secret wishes to break out and be bad.

Feigning delight, I gave Mom breakfast in bed, chose her reading material at the library, and tucked her into bed at night with a Valium. Then, after my devoted daughter bit, I'd sneak out of the house and drive her car, fantasizing that I was eighteen and leaving for good, sometimes having thoughts that she might crash in it the next time she came home from work. Beyond this facade was my fantasy world, a happy place where I was fabulous and endless possibilities existed.

I became a good/bad girl. My job was to have the house clean when my mother got home from work. The bad girl would wait until fifteen minutes before she was due. The good girl, fueled by my fantasies, would set the oven timer for 10 minutes and pretend that if the house was clean when the timer went off, I would win a trip to Disneyland. I cleaned furiously, and if I got done in time I didn't get beaten. Sometimes Mom would come home early and blow up at me. I then castigated myself for not starting the cleaning earlier so as to spare myself the pain.

The Bad Daughter

But I couldn't stop walking too close to the fire. Even getting frequently burned was preferable to following the rules. Following the rules felt like killing off the last little bit of me. I still craved contact, any contact, from my mother—especially the kind my brother was getting. Darrell had hearing problems from an early age, surgery to correct his adenoids, and diabetes. I watched Mom pour devotional care upon my brother. She sent little attention my way unless she was angry; I was there to help her take care of Darrell.

So numb were my feelings that the thrill of reckless daring was one of the few I still registered. I cut school frequently, forged report cards for myself and my friends, and smoked my mother's cigarettes in the bathtub. Whenever I got caught breaking rules, I portrayed a good girl overly influenced by friends. But behind this good/bad split and the thrill of the "bad" part was a growing belief that my mother was right: I was even worse than weak—I was inherently evil.

I felt a growing need to become a good, strong person. It was too soon for me to know that my whole premise was faulty, for I had not been introduced to any other ways of thinking or seeing myself. I started a quest for God, thinking that maybe He could make me be a good person. My God at that time was a big strong Daddy in the sky. My mother was antireligion and resented God for giving her a raw deal, but she didn't stop me from going to whatever church was nearby. We moved a lot, so I went to a lot of churches—Catholic, Presbyterian, Baptist, Mormon—and even to Jewish synagogues. My multitude of experiences confused me. I thought, *How is hearing what a sinner I am, coloring pictures of Jesus, and reciting the books of the Bible going to make me be a good person? Where is God?*

An elder at the Mormon church asked me to give a testimonial about why I believed. I said I couldn't because I didn't believe yet, I just really wanted to believe. The next Sunday, the elder gave a testimonial about a young person with a depth of faith that inspired him. I thought, *I need this person to inspire me too.* Then he introduced me as that faithful person. I was stunned into quitting the church. In my mind, I was still a bad person. He, a good man of God, had lied to his congregation about me.

So I stopped trying to believe in God, and launched another good girl/bad girl series of events—stealing clothes from department stores and giving them, along with all my toys, to the children who lived next door. At the times when I felt thoroughly ashamed, for stealing or for desperately seeking attention, I would increase my striving for goodness.

We moved so much that I went to sixteen schools, including five high schools. I was always the new girl. Although armored with false confidence, I didn't know how to fit in when I started at a new school. I always felt that my hair and clothes were wrong. By the time I figured out what was cool, I was already in the next school. My inability to reach out for friendship left me with the friends who chose *me*—usually the bad girls. Drama and choir were my only sanctuaries.

Juvenile Hall

Three weeks after meeting him, my mother married her third husband. Problems between Elmer and Mom surfaced immediately, and they blamed me for the tension in their marriage. If I weren't such a bad daughter, they could be happy together. I was put on restriction until further notice. When I defied the "grounding," I ended up in Juvenile Hall, labeled an 'incorrigible.' Even there, my fantasies reigned. I considered myself some kind of journalist sent to do a story on the place. Strangely, Juvenile Hall was a good experience for me. The baddest of the bad girls took a liking to me, which strengthened my sense of security. I was smarter and more facile than most, and began to feel a little bit of real confidence.

One night I sang in my cell right after lights-out. I sang "Summertime," and was surprised by the sound of my voice. I sang easily, as I had when I was with Grandma, and the words of the song made me feel less locked up. Because my mother didn't like high voices, I had always hated that I was a soprano. But that night the sound of my voice comforted me. The next night, the girls in the Hall asked me to sing again, louder. In the month that I was there, I sang nearly every night, which was a healing for me. Whenever I had sung at home, Mom had told me to shut up.

I became a ward of the court, and went to live in a foster home. This was my new chance to be a strong, good person. Judith, divorced and only twenty-eight, was my foster parent. Her boyfriend, Harry, was an attorney who helped her get custody of me. On the drive from Juvenile Hall to my new home, my life changed again. When Harry paid the toll at the entrance to the San Rafael bridge, he gave a friendly "Hello, how are you?" to the toll taker. I was stunned, as my mother would never have done this. She believed in never acknowledging strangers—or even talking to neighbors—because they might "want something from you." I began to study Harry's ways: his friendliness, the time he took with people, and the genuine interest he showed in Judith and me.

Harry was my first real role model. He taught me about the concept of excellence, which to me meant being the best I could be. He reinforced my hope of becoming honest and motivated. The people in Harry's world were achievers who had reached a level of mastery and success that fascinated and compelled me. I wanted to be one of them. Meanwhile, I was not happy living with Judith and didn't want to stay with her. She disapproved of my boyfriend, Chris, and wanted me to see other boys. I refused.

A Teenage Marriage

I adored Chris, and saw him as my hero. With him, I had my first sexual experiences. I became pregnant, and he married me of his own volition—against the will of both of our mothers. Chris's mother was incensed that I wore white at our wedding, because I wasn't a virgin. In the receiving line at our reception, she cried as she hugged her son, then walked by me without a word. I was seventeen; he was nearly twenty.

I believe that Chris and I really loved each other, but we didn't know how to show it. We were great friends who could talk about any subject except our relationship. We were too young to have learned anything about communication, autonomy, or intimacy. I felt love through verbal expression and displays of emotion, but Chris was unable to give those things. He felt love through sexual expression, but I was sexually repressed.

My history with my stepfather had left me susceptible to feeling like a sex object. When that old attitude was triggered, I froze and couldn't feel pleasure in my body. I felt unloved and sexually exploited by my husband, though I now know that this was a misperception. Chris dictated my choices like a stern father. I felt that I'd had more freedom when I was ten years old than I had with him. When I complained about how unfair he was, he either turned a deaf ear or made me laugh. He could always make me laugh, no matter how angry I was. I still regret that I could never let Chris know that he was the most important person in the world to me.

Our son, also named Chris, was born on Labor Day. Even though I was totally unprepared to be a mother, Chris's birth was my first visit to heaven since being with my grandmother. When I first saw my child, I felt waves of gratitude that this could really be happening to me.

My mother and Elmer had been divorced after nine months of marriage, and she and I had tried many times to reconcile our relationship. When Chris was born, she came to help me, but was so overwhelmed that I had to take care of both her and the baby.

Soon, the elder Chris and I decided to move to Hawaii, where his family lived. The night before we left, we had friends over to help us pack. Mom appeared, drunk and ranting. She picked up a table and threw it at the TV. My husband had a real talent for understatement. He snatched the table out of the air before it hit the TV and set it down as if nothing had happened. This infuriated Mom even more, for she needed to make an impact. She said to my husband, in front of the others, "Do you know what your wife's problem is? My husband was screwing her for years."

I rose from my chair, and out of me came a voice that I had never heard before. "You liar!" I shouted again and again, as I dragged my mother out onto the balcony. I had raised her off the ground as if she weighed nothing when, in my peripheral vision, I saw my husband leaning in his "It's cool" way against the house. His presence balanced me. Instead of pushing Mom off our second-floor balcony, I threw her down and shook her by her hair as she had done so many times to me, until Chris gently pulled me away from her.

The next morning, we took some promised furniture to my mother's house. I looked into her room, where she was in bed, bruised and hung over. Mom said, "I'm sorry I said what I did. I wanted to say what would hurt you the most."

"That was it," I retorted, still angry.

Mom came back with, "You are no longer a daughter of mine."

I agreed. "Deal—because you never were a mother to me!"

We didn't speak for nearly two years. After many subsequent reconciliations and separations, we have yet to really clear the air. When I look back to that time, I think my mother found the only way she could to express the sadness she felt about my moving away.

6

Challenging
My Perfectionism

I had built a huge romantic fantasy around living in Hawaii, and of course the reality was different. For the first several months we were there, the three of us lived with my mother-in-law, who still disapproved of me, and Chris's five siblings, in a house with one bathroom. Even though I felt like an outsider, this was my first real experience of family. My in-laws welcomed me as much as they could, and completely adored young Chris. Although I was desperate to belong, I felt both suffocated and unbearably lonely. I couldn't hold myself in my marriage; it felt too much like a prison. I had to break out.

The day I told Chris I wanted a separation was the day he first showed me any real emotion. I think he would have worked to make our marriage better, but I had passed the point of no return, for I had waited too long to let him know how serious I thought our problems were. I had pretended to be happy when I was really miserable. When our marriage ended after two and one-half years. I still had not learned how to tell the truth.

Chris vowed that he would fight for custody of our son, saying, "Hawaii is not a woman's state—the mother doesn't automatically get the child." His income was higher than mine, and his family certainly more stable and better able to provide for a child. I feared a court would not judge in my favor. Feeling that I didn't deserve to keep my son, I stole him away from his father. I fled Hawaii, landing in San Francisco with $30, no car, no job, and no place to live. I was twenty; my son was barely two. Though I felt like a criminal for putting him into such an insecure situation, I had to keep him with me at all costs.

Chris followed us to California and showed up at the place where we were staying, with a male friend to help him take little Chris away from me. I turned into a mother lioness, blocking the front door so they wouldn't take him. Chris's friend quickly reassessed the situation, and instead of helping my husband take my son from me, he calmed him down. After they had gone, leaving young Chris with me, I felt as if I should have let my son go, as if I had no right to keep him.

Single Parenthood

The next couple of years were hard. I went on welfare for a year, and lived in a fog of fear and depression that I didn't recognize until years later, when I felt safe enough to look back. Chris's father returned to California to be close to his son, and became involved with someone he had known in high school. They married, and have been together ever since.

Motherhood became no easier for me, nor did childhood get any easier for my son. Chris was a handful. Although he was very sweet-natured, he was all boy. I could manage neither him nor my overwhelming sense of inadequacy. I had no clue how to give him what he needed . . . I only knew I had to be different from the way my mother was with me. I didn't want to hit him, though I did a few times and felt dreadful about it. I told him I loved him because I remembered how much I had needed to hear that from Mom. But I was unable to give him all the attention and affection he needed.

One evening at dusk, I saw Chris walking home from day care, carrying his school work. I could barely see him approaching me in the distance. It seemed too dark for a six-year-old to be walking down the street by himself. I felt a wave of sorrow that my son had me for a mother. By the time Chris was eight, I had reached a height of self-loathing, and I agreed to let him live with his father and see me only on weekends.

Pushing the Limits

My life became a race for peak experiences, with ever-changing jobs and relationships—all of it revolving around drugs and alcohol. Yet I remained in denial of this. To notice might have meant being consumed by the inner voice that believed I was weak and evil. My bursts of effort were followed by backlashes of depression. Though I had sworn that I would never follow in my mother's and stepfather's footsteps, I worked as a bartender for several years. In my self-destructiveness and empty arrogance, I grew hard, and developed a caustic sense of humor that was applauded by the bar customers for its entertainment value.

I buried my sense of innocence, while strengthening my armor of tough cynicism. I stole from one of the bars, right under the manager's nose while we were talking together. When I discovered how well I could bluff my opponents, gambling became a favorite way to supplement my income. For a time, I was the angel on the arm of a drug dealer, joining him on his night drops to athletes, rock stars, Hell's Angels, and high school principals. Sex became another way to push the limits of experience. I sought as many different kinds of sexual adventure as I could imagine. These experiments, though very dangerous, were necessary for me. I needed to test my power, imagination, and limitations in some way. To separate my strengths from my weaknesses and find my place to stand, I had to push every boundary I encountered. I needed to know, *How capable am I of creation? Of destruction? What's inside of me that could kill me? What's inside of me that could save me?*

A Dream of Chinese Women

A vivid dream in 1975 served as my turning point. I was at a party on the night before a trip to Mainland China. My friends toasted my departure with liqueur from an antique bottle they had recently purchased. There were carvings of ancient Chinese women on the bottle. As I poured the liqueur into glasses, I cut my hand where one of the carvings was chipped. Then I was on a crowded street in China. From the direction opposite of where I was headed with my friends, a group of beautiful Chinese women in ancient costume headed toward me. I got engulfed in the group and swept in their direction. I realized that these women were being herded by men, as if they were cattle. The women approached me, and I saw that they were as ancient as their costumes. They looked at me with such ferocious intensity that I got the feeling they wanted to kill and consume me. I broke away and ran.

Then I was in my hotel, where a British man with sandy-colored hair and a handlebar mustache came to my room. He told me he had been sent by a Chinese healer, to inform me that I had been cursed and must come to him right away. Then I was with the Chinese man, who was so old that his teeth looked loose and wooden. He spoke no English, but I understood him through the clacking sounds he made with his teeth. He told me he couldn't save me—that I must find my own way to discover and break the curse, or I would die. He gave me herbs for clarity and to ease my pain while I struggled with this challenge.

Then I was back in California, inside a massive library—an archive of ancient knowledge. I knew that I must search this library to learn how to break my curse. I walked out of the library and stood at the top of its front steps, looking at a small park across the street. The Chinese women were together there, waiting for me. I felt fear that I was going to die young.

All the messages and symbolism in this dream were completely lost on me, but the dream planted a seed in my unconscious that started me thinking about finding a new way to live. I quit drinking, smoking, and taking drugs, and enrolled in hairdressing school so as to leave the bar life, fast. But profound change doesn't happen fast, and the gravity of my old ways kept pulling me down.

Stopped in My Tracks

I married a sweet and soulful man, Stacey, who said that he too wanted to move toward a new life. But Stacey had his own inner demons, which had plans of their own. Our relationship was volatile, as we each looked to the other for rescue. I wanted him to help me find a healthy new way to live. He hoped that the strength of my love would lift him above his darkness. Instead, we took each other down.

Life finally stopped me in my tracks. I became ill, with constant flu-like symptoms for which conventional medicine could do nothing. The physicians I saw couldn't diagnose my illness, so they said it was psychosomatic and sent me to psychiatrists. I was sick for a year, which gave me an unprecedented opportunity to ponder my predicament and change my approach to life. During that time, it was all I could do to drag myself through a day's work and return home to sleep. All my vitality and my sense of humor vanished, and I became deeply depressed. The situation was eerily reminiscent of my dream of the Chinese women. I knew I had to do something miraculous to save myself.

New Beginnings

During this time, I was not yet ready to see how broken and fragile I was, but I was ready to question my past choices and behavior. I was ready to begin taking care of myself through diet, exercise, and natural health remedies, and ready to leave my marriage, for I believed that it couldn't take me where I needed to go. I started a business—a unisex hair salon—near the bars where I had worked. In the salon, I stocked a full bar, and I promised a free drink to any of my old customers who could pry themselves off the bar stool long enough to come in for a haircut. They came, and my business thrived. It was a time of proving myself to myself and starting to build a new life.

Throughout my life, my relationships with women had been poor. They didn't like me—sometimes because of envy, but often because I was unapproachable in manner and I never approached them. This dynamic was turned around in the salon, as all the woman who entered were treated like guests in my home and all of my effort and talent was given to them. Vanity ruled my life in those days: the salon focus was about feeling better through looking better. The folly of that approach never occurred to us, for we failed to notice how unhappy we were even with perfect hair and makeup.

I observed some of my female clients struggling with their relationships to themselves, striving to attain physical perfection. Many behaved as if their hair were an evil alien living atop their head and the objective was to beat it into submission. Some women left my clientele in search of the perfect hairdresser who could boost their self-esteem by perfecting their appearance. Fortunately, I learned early on to let them come and go without taking offense. I knew they often returned once they learned there was no magical silver bullet that could fix them inside, through the outside. Over two years, this lesson gradually dawned on me, too, and running a hair business finally lost its meaning for me. I sold the salon, to begin a new quest for inner peace and a sense of purpose.

Facing My Fears

Fear was my biggest crippler, my excuse to not fully live my life. I was starting to like myself enough to want to do something about that. I began reading books about the inner journey and about facing fears that live in the mind. One of the books said that you don't have to do anything special to face fear; just sit still and it will arise. I took a class in meditation, and became hell-bent on sitting still and facing my fear.

I holed up in my apartment for what turned out to be three weeks. During that time, my monsters from the deep rose up to truly terrify me. I closed my eyes to sleep at night and saw an evil-looking face with red-rimmed eyes leering at me. I drew the face in my journal. Nightmares woke me during the night. I described them in my journal. A leaf falling to the floor from one of my plants startled me awake. My phone rang and a strange voice screamed obscenities at me. I turned off the bell on my phone, and put the answering machine in the refrigerator.

While meditating, I heard cracking sounds in the walls and thought they were a message for me. I felt vibrations and surges of energy in my body. Sometimes I left my body and floated around near the ceiling. At other times I sensed a presence in the room with me, and alternated between trying to make it go away and trying to feel comfortable just letting it be there. A few times I saw, in my mind's eye, a reaching hand and arm that I named The Grim Reaper, because it seemed like the hand of death. I thought, *If I'm going crazy, I will let it happen and believe I can find my way back to sanity. If I'm dying, I will let that happen and believe that I can be reborn.* I no longer wanted to live in fear of myself and in fear of life.

According to the psychological perspective, I had post-traumatic stress disorder from my childhood abuse. I thought, *If that is so, I will ride it to its conclusion.* What felt more accurate was that I was having a spiritual crisis between the part of me that wanted to live and the part of me that wanted to shrivel and die.

After three weeks, I felt a calm and a clearing within me. I now felt safe enough on the inside to face a few fears on the outside. I was not afraid of myself anymore, but I was still afraid of the world and most of the people in it. I decided to do what scared me the most: take a trip on my own.

Mexico is not considered a good place for women to travel alone, especially if you don't know the language. This made it perfect for my purposes. My plan was to go there and face more fear, to conquer shyness through struggling to communicate in a foreign language, to turn scary strangers into friends, and perhaps to retrieve a little of my personal power. I took two books with me as guides: *Tales of Power* by Carlos Castaneda and a more obscure one about connecting to an inner teacher, by an author whose name I can't remember. I knew I had barely begun my inner journey, and I wanted to bring my inner and outer worlds together. I went to Mexico City, visited remote towns, learned a little Spanish, meditated at many of the ruins and pyramids, met people from all over the world, and broke through to another level of feeling alive and free inside my own skin.

A Teacher and a Mission

I could a feel a new strength inside, but I still didn't know what to do with myself. I still craved a deeper sense of purpose. That was when I met the man that I will simply call my teacher. I heard that he gave trainings in inner guidance, and the mention of those words ignited me. Inner guidance was exactly what I wanted. I immediately enrolled in his course, and the experience of it blessed me with the sense of purpose I had been seeking for so long. I began to feel a solidity and an at-homeness inside myself that I had not felt since being held in the arms of my beloved grandmother. It was a spiritual awakening that my arrogance soon latched onto, telling me I had discovered the secret of life itself.

I had found God again (though I wouldn't say that word in those days), and now I had a mission: to take inner guidance to the world. After several months of training, I enrolled in a very challenging one-year course to become an inner-guidance teacher. I felt a dedication to my studies that I had never before experienced. My teacher generously fed my starved ego, which made me feel special. I felt devoted to him because he was devoted to inner guidance, and I saw him as empowering people to trust themselves.

Soon a group of six adult students moved to a spiritual retreat in the mountains with my teacher, his wife, and their son. I sold or gave away most of my belongings, and off we went. Once we were there, my teacher gave us instructions to follow. Most of these seemed relevant to our development as teachers of inner guidance, but some felt counter to the direction in which my own inner guidance was leading me.

We were there for ten months. For seven of those months, we withdrew completely from the world and totally immersed ourselves into relating with each other. Our guidelines required us to refrain from any reading, listening to the radio, watching movies or television, or engaging in independent activities. I was breakfast cook, typist of new curriculum, and general house manager. We strictly adhered to our meditation practice. Conflict was rampant, and we processed and resolved it as a community. Following my marriage to Chris, this retreat served as my next (and most intense) family experience. It was the first time I had ever surrendered my individuality for the good of the group.

At the end of the retreat, each of us was sent to a different city to establish the inner-guidance training in that location. I went to Oregon for ten months, and then on to Los Angeles. This two-year period was extremely hard for me. I didn't know people in these areas, and to start trainings from scratch required meeting new people and giving public talks. I was scared, yet buoyed by my feeling of having a mission.

Confronting My Perfectionist

The students in my trainings were teachers, ministers, psychotherapists, and educators, most of whom had done more personal inner work than I had done. As they were learning about spiritual development from me, I was learning about personal development from them, and discovering how much I didn't know.

During this period, it gradually dawned on me that, though I was freer than I had ever been, my mind was still not my own. I felt a growing rift between my teacher's instruction and my own inner guidance. His was a closed community, and to remain within its sanctuary, one had to obey his guidelines. However, I had taken the "inner" guidance part so much to heart that I could no longer follow my teacher's lessons. I felt that life had withdrawn its sanction for me to be an inner-guidance teacher. I had to strengthen my relationship to inner guidance and win more of my personal freedom before I'd be truly ready to empower others to do the same for themselves. I saw no need to discard all the good things the inner-guidance training had given me, but I had to leave the organization.

I had continued to get sick for weeks or months at a time, and I still didn't know why. People continually told me that I was too hard on myself, but I didn't believe them. I thought I was not hard enough, and didn't know why I couldn't "just do it." I didn't know why most of my gains were followed by loss of interest, lack of follow-through or rebellious backlashes, and then depression. I didn't know why I couldn't stop opposing my own efforts. I had hit a wall in my work.

I sensed that, inside of me, something major was still missing. My students had unknowingly shown me that I still had empty spaces and wounded places within that many of them had already filled and healed. I suspected that there was something wrong in the way I thought and behaved that was making me sick and depressed. I wanted to find out what it was and change it. It occurred to me that, in my earnest search for true Inner Guidance, I was still misguided.

I realized that something inside of me that had been presenting itself as my voice of Inner Guidance actually sounded more like an angry parent—my own angry parent! Although I had been long out of her house, my enraged mother was still inside my head, louder than ever— pushing me and criticizing my every thought and move. I then further realized that it wasn't just my mother inside my head—the demanding voice sounded and felt like God. The deity of my present understanding was still an angry parent, a God that my fearful self had formulated to help me survive my life, a God who believed He was helping me by preventing me from being weak and bad and turning me into someone strong and good. His plan was to save my life by pushing me to achieve perfection.

Giving Up My Need to Be Good

Instead of choosing the path of Inner Guidance, I had been following an urgency to obey my mother and my unfriendly God. I saw that I was no freer than when I had been trapped in rebelliousness. Instead of being bad, I was now stuck in my efforts to be good, and still subject to backlashes of being bad. I really wanted to get off this good/bad, bad/ good track. But I found that it was not that easy. Hard as I tried, I kept underestimating my task and misunderstanding the process of change. The old behavior kept reappearing. I began to realize that there would be many more struggles with my good/bad split.

I had the following positive realization: *I am worthy enough right now, if I never change another thing. I don't have to banish all of my bad qualities before I can move forward in my life. I can live now.* I began to accept the continual job of reminding myself to release my need to be good.

My new goal was to be healthy and to live a full life, yet my increasing wisdom told me to prepare for many more slips. I wanted to find faith in myself—not instead of doubt, but in spite of it. I felt ready and willing to do all the necessary personal work in front of me. I needed to find more compassion for my faults and weaknesses, and more internal permission to learn from my mistakes. Trying to be perfect had made me sick. I felt determined to let myself be a human being, no better or worse than anyone else.

In order to find a less "perfect" and more human way, I had to face my self-destructive behaviors and the ways in which I was weak. All my previous attempts to change myself had been acts of self-rejection that had further weakened me. To give up perfectionism would not mean rushing blindly to create change. It would mean making changes from a feeling of goodwill toward myself.

Before I could begin to change anything, I wanted to know more of the components of my predicament. I began a deep process of self-observation and study. I watched and listened intently to everyone who came into view. The best way for me to begin to understand my challenge was to separate out and distinguish between the different parts of myself. Conflict is the tension of opposing forces, and I was riddled with it.

My Opposing Inner Forces

Motivated by a wish to bridge psychology and spirituality, I enrolled in school to become a psychotherapist. To locate and fill in the missing or mixed-up parts of my psyche, I also went into personal therapy. I discovered that there are two potent opposing forces within me. The first, which I was eventually to call the Perfectionist, values only "doing." It pushes me, prods me, and drives me into self-doubt, then tries to pull me out of it. It tells me I'm in trouble, that I'm unequal to the task, that I will fail at all I attempt. It assures me that its intention is to direct me to redemption. The other force, to which I eventually gave the name of Helpless, is a kind of inertia. It feels as if it never wants to do anything ever again; it just wants to be left alone. But it is very strong, and it is capable of lashing out if threatened.

I decided that, in order to dismantle my overbearing "doer," I had to know it thoroughly. I needed to see it in action, feel it, and name it. I sensed that it was not all bad, that it was simply energy misapplied. I wanted to sort through all its parts to separate the helpful ones from the harmful ones, and then I wanted to nail the harmful ones.

Originally, I named my perfectionism The Grim Reaper, because it felt like the bony hand of death that had repeatedly shown itself to me when I locked myself away to face my fear. The Grim Reaper represented the consequences of my fear in action. It was indeed killing me, but that didn't quite sum up my experience of it. Yes, it was fear, and—yes—it felt like a killer, but it killed slowly, by gripping me till I felt strangled and smothered. When I was in its clutches, my body clamped itself down in anxiety. So I shortened The Grim Reaper to The Gripper. Later still, I gave it the more comprehensive name that it still bears.

The Perfectionist is one part of an ongoing conversation inside of me—the part that says, *You can't*. The part of me it is talking to is its counterpart, which listens and says, *You're right, I can't*. The Perfectionist attacks by applying pressure and criticism. The other side feels the pressure, grows anxious and depressed, and eventually is exhausted by the one who says with such conviction, *You're nothing without me. Trust only me to help you.* Feeling the sheer force of the message, the other side of the conversation believes, and responds, *Yes, please help me. I can't do anything without you. I am yours to command.*

The hyperaggression of perfectionism is a form of tyranny, fixed in fear and rejection, in which the task, goal, or project is considered more important than the person or the process. My Perfectionist pushes with an urgent, doubt-driven force. If it targets me, I become exhausted. If it targets you, you become exhausted. Once I had seen my Perfectionist for what it is, I knew I could no longer live under its domination. If I never accomplished another single thing, I needed to find the place within me where I value and approve of myself.

Time Off From Ambition

My initial response to my new perspective was to declare war on the Perfectionist—to beat it into the ground. I vowed I would never let it treat me harshly again. Before long, I recognized that my warrior approach was me employing the Perfectionist to defeat the Perfectionist. Perfectionism cannot be opposed harshly, for that only strengthens it. Force, toughness, and severity all come from the Perfectionist, and cannot be used against it. No use fighting fire with fire.

Perfectionism is deceptive. Even writing about it now is like stepping into quicksand. In my efforts to beat it, I kept crashing into myself. So I decided not to allow myself to respond to any feeling of pressure or pushing. I would only let myself follow pleasure and aliveness.

My ambition vanished. My former commitment to excellence and achievement meant nothing to me. I could barely read a book. As time passed, my friends began to worry about me. I had been known as the one who gets things done, who inspires everyone else to excellence. Focus and speed had been my specialty. I had gotten my therapy license, built a thriving private practice, and knocked off my Ph.D., all in record-breaking time.

Now my time was spent sitting and staring at the sky, or gazing at trees and flowers. When I wanted to move, I would walk in the hills with my dogs, or sing and dance for my own pleasure. I wanted to be Winnie the Pooh. My friends, or the Perfectionists in my friends, saw this as trouble. So did my own Perfectionist. *Uh oh*, it thought, *maybe I'll never finish writing my book. Maybe I've really fallen apart this time. What do I do now? Have I hit the heights of rationalization for laziness?*

But another voice suggested that maybe this was the most important time of all to trust myself, and to just wait. To not move an inch, if the reason I'd be moving would be just because I thought I should. To dare to wait until I noticed myself move spontaneously, and then notice what I was moving toward.

The operative word is "notice." The Perfectionist tells me I could get stuck waiting for the rest of my life. *Yes, that's true*, I respond, *if I sleep while I wait*. But it's not true if, while I wait, I keenly notice myself. When first awakening in the morning, I notice an ongoing struggle with myself about how to start the day. I used to not want to wake up and deal with that struggle. My Perfectionist used to tell me I couldn't even wake up right: *It's already late. Hurry up! There's so much to do.* So I would push myself, moving through molasses to get out of bed.

Even now I am not free of perfectionism. I don't think we ever are, nor is that even the goal. As of this writing, my goal is to learn how to live with myself, which includes learning how to relate to my perfectionism. These days, when I wake up, I begin to notice my experience of being in a new day. I will not get out of bed until my body starts to move without being pushed. That means there is something my body wants to move toward.

Sometimes it starts by moving from a lying position to a sitting position. Then I let my eyes tell me when they want to open. Then I notice I am moving, unbidden, out of the bed. This seems like exceedingly remedial work, and it is remedial, because my weakest link needs this much attention. If I am refusing to drag myself through life anymore, I have to find and free the part of me that is a drag.

Too much of my life has been spent either doing or fighting against doing. This is not so for my role model, Winnie the Pooh, who just is. He maintains a natural balance of being and doing without even thinking about it. Now, I can't realistically ask myself to just "be" because I am too tangled in my past experiences. So, to find the place inside that will allow me to be, I have to untangle myself.

The most noticeable part of this process is my feelings, which can be pretty unmanageable. If I fail to notice them, they lead me to some very scary places. But if I do notice them, and steady myself as I feel them instead of acting them out, they help me to untangle my perfectionism.

Although feelings can cause pure havoc if they are avoided, it took me a long time to learn that they are not the be-all and end-all of my process. If I pay attention to them, they lead me to the truth that lies beyond feelings. My teacher once told me, "You must know what you feel before you can feel what you know."

I now know how to call upon the fund of wisdom from which comes my Inner Guidance. The Perfectionist still tries to be my Inner Guidance, but I now know that it is not. I know because I can feel the difference.

Although my story doesn't end here, I am happy to say that the results of my perfectionism recovery process have clearly manifested in my life. Most of my demons continue to dwell within me, but they are minor pests now and rarely interfere with my living or loving.

I now know something that I didn't know before: that I can make happen whatever I can imagine, which includes good health, achievement, adventure, and, of course, love. I said to my Love the other day that I used to be terrified of myself and the world. Now, I'm at home in myself, and the world feels like a peach ripe for the picking.

7

When Two Perfectionists Collide

What if your boss, your co-worker, your spouse, or your child is also a perfectionist? Imagine a collision between two cars, each one going at 60 miles per hour. The impact is measured at 120 miles per hour. When dealing with another perfectionist, if you do not moderate your own perfectionism, any conflict will be twice as difficult to settle. The Perfectionist is hard, and rigidly set in its ways. The only response to its severity that may help is softness, which is not to be confused with submissiveness.

The Perfectionist is frightened, but usually doesn't know it. It needs to be calmed, soothed, and made to feel safe before it can listen to reason. If you find yourself in combat with a perfectionist, look first for your own. If you are feeling right, angry, not trusted, disrespected, misunderstood, the person you are fighting is probably feeling the same way. The one who needs to yield is the one who sees the necessity for yielding. "Yes, but I'm right and I always have to be the one to give in," is a natural response. But you are not being asked to give in. You are being asked to soften your own hardness and look for another way to resolve the conflict.

There are many ways to prevail over the Perfectionist, whether it's yours or somebody else's, but fighting it head-on isn't one of them. When locked in a conflict, the Perfectionist is deaf, dumb, and blind to reason. It can hear nothing other than, "You're right. We'll do it your way. I understand you. I trust you. I respect you. I want what you want."

That message can be truthfully conveyed without an unconditional surrender. Remember that perfectionism is triggered by the onset of a threat, and that even the most severe perfectionists are not always caught in their perfectionism. But before we can reason with the individual, it is necessary to remove the threat and thus disarm the Perfectionist.

The Underdog in a Rock Band

A client of mine that we'll call Joe was the bass player for a veteran pop star that we'll call Ronnie. They had played and written songs together for more than ten years, and during that time they had developed a full-fledged but unspoken rivalry.

Joe felt disrespected, unappreciated, and outpowered by Ronnie's inflated ego, and he would get sulky and morose about it. Ronnie felt judged by Joe as not real or soulful enough, which only increased his show of bravado. Each was stuck in a state of needing the other's approval. Joe had a self-deprecating way of seeking the approval, and Ronnie had an arrogant way.

One factor that Joe had to accept was that, no matter what approach he chose, he could not threaten Ronnie's "top dog" position. If he wanted to stay in the band, he would have to remain as a subordinate to the band's star. He decided that he wanted to stay for at least a while longer.

An ongoing conflict between them happened when Ronnie was nervous before a performance and would begin to make nit-picky criticisms of Joe's guitar playing. This was Ronnie's Perfectionist's way of making sure he would get the best performance out of Joe. But the effect it had on Joe was that he felt his legs cut out from under him, and started each performance with hurt feelings.

If Joe told Ronnie that he felt disrespected, unappreciated, and outpowered, that message would trigger Ronnie's Perfectionist even more and Joe would end up feeling more outpowered than ever. He needed to approach Ronnie with the message (but not the direct words), "I know that you respect me and appreciate me, and that you have the power." His approach needed to also take into consideration Ronnie's sore spot about not feeling as real or soulful as Joe.

Considering how many times this conflict had repeated itself over the years, Joe had plenty of time to plan, study, practice, and improve his strategy. The process of his interaction with Ronnie could be broken down into stages. The first stage was realizing that there was a rivalry going on between them. Then he needed to hear the unspoken communication beneath the spoken words. It took some time for him to really know how he felt, and then he needed to study Ronnie, as well, to learn how Ronnie must feel during these conflicts.

Then Joe needed to observe his own knee-jerk responses to Ronnie's arrogance. Rarely did Joe say anything out loud, but his sulky manner told his rival that Ronnie had done something wrong. Ronnie had no choice but to fill in the mysterious void of Joe's unhappiness with the contents of his own insecurity: the fear that he was not genuine enough, and that Joe was a deeper-feeling man than he.

Before Joe was ready to respond differently to Ronnie, he had to watch himself act out his old pattern of sulking and think about what he could do differently to cause a different outcome for both of them. After studying their interactions for a while, Joe began to comprehend the dynamic that they were both caught in. Now it was time for him to rehearse in his mind some new behavior.

Taking a New Approach With the Top Dog

His thought process went something like this: *As long as I want to stay in the band, I need to approach Ronnie with a certain amount of allegiance. This doesn't mean that he's a better person than I am. It means that he's the boss, and wants to be treated as such.*

Ronnie's criticism may actually have nothing to do with me. It may only be coming from his insecurity. When he criticizes me before a performance, what might it mean besides the meaning I give to it from my own insecurity, which tells me that I'm not worthy of respect or appreciation, and—even worse—that I'm powerless?

These factors needed to be addressed on their own, of course, not just in the context of Joe's interactions with Ronnie. Once he had explored his own insecurity, Joe saw that it was at the core of all of his conflicts. He then decided to make Ronnie his "practice person," with whom he would win a sense of self-respect and appreciation and a feeling of personal power. He realized that those elements were the very ones he needed to claim in order to quit the band and strike out on his own. When he mastered this conflict with Ronnie, he would have "graduated," and he would be free to go.

Joe knew what his messages to Ronnie now needed to convey: "You are the boss. I know that you respect and appreciate me, because I feel the same way about you. I know that your comments before a performance are made just to ensure that you get the best possible performance out of your band." In other words: "You're a good guy and you've done nothing wrong."

This is the ground upon which we can ask someone to do something differently than they usually do it. But the message has to be implied; it cannot be stated directly. If we are to keep the Perfectionist from feeling threatened, humiliated, or out of control, we need to address its fears without directly exposing them.

So Joe's message needed to be conveyed through attitude and tone of voice, and it needed to address Ronnie's need in that moment, which was getting the best performance. It was this approach that would coax Ronnie to pay attention and perhaps even to be willing to change. The message was: "I understand what you want, and this is how you can get it."

Putting an End to the Conflict

It is imperative, when we're dealing with someone else's perfectionism, to let their Perfectionist feel that it is still in control. Over the course of the next few performances, Joe was able to gently inform Ronnie how he could elicit his bass player's best performance. It would have been unrealistic for him to think he could reverse such a long-established pattern in a single encounter. It took several conversations, with small inroads made in each one.

Joe couldn't tell Ronnie what not to say; he had to tell him what to say. And he had to reveal himself a bit, to soften Ronnie. It went something like this: "You know, Ronnie, I've never really let you know how nervous I get before a performance. I don't want to feel that way anymore. I've been looking for different ways to get psyched before we play. If you have any thoughts or words that could boost me over that first hurdle, that would be very cool."

Joe had to swallow some of his pride to say these words and mean them, but they worked. Ronnie gradually went from criticizing him and the other band members before a performance, to inspiring them before a performance. Joe's win helped equalize the competition he felt with Ronnie, and took the edge off their rivalry. The risk he took to change this particular dynamic had far-reaching consequences. It gave him the confidence and sense of personal power that he needed in order to quit the band. Joe moved on to become a successful recording artist with his own band.

The Perfectionist is a warrior that will fight to the bitter end. When allowed to go to its extreme, it may quit jobs, end friendships, fire a favorite employee, leave a marriage, or disown a child before it will admit defeat or stop to consider its actions.

When in conflict with another person, even if we disagree on every point we can still convey messages to soften the opposing perfectionist. This will allow the person behind it to come out and continue the negotiation in a more reasonable fashion. When dealing with perfectionists who need to be right, our way can prevail—as long as we don't need to be right, too.

8

The Process of Recovery

A fter we have begun to uncover our specific type of perfectionism
and its consequences (illness, depression, addiction, loneliness,
anxiety), it is time to ask: "Do I want Inner Guidance enough to take the
cure from perfectionism?" To enter into a recovery process will require
the strength of commitment; it is not a challenge to be accepted lightly.
Our commitment to recovery can disappear unless we continually
remember the rewards we're going after and feel a strong desire for
them.

I still consider myself to be in the recovery process. Relief from the
consequences of perfectionism is not enough for me. I want to be free
from the cause of my perfectionism. I want to live outside my fears, not
inside them. I want to feel free to contribute, to express myself. I want
to be less self-conscious in my loving.

Whenever I have to recommit to my recovery from perfectionism,
I stop to remember what it is I'm after. When I'm porch sittin' at eighty-
five, I want to look back and know that I lived a full life. Once I have
remembered this goal, then my challenge is to awaken to the opposition
that lurks within my mind.

Accepting the Challenge to Awaken

When we prepare well and enter willingly, the thrill of the inner
world is no less than that of the African bush. In fact, the African
walking safari that I experienced with six other women is my metaphor
for the awakening process.

The land was harsh and the walking rigorous. The bush was thick with ruts, stumps, insects, vines, poisonous snakes, low-slung tree branches, piles of animal droppings, and countless varieties of thorns. We had to pay close attention or suffer injury. Our guide said that, to ensure survival, we had to be switched-on: awake, aware, and in the moment. Had I not anticipated some hardship, and had I not been emotionally prepared for a rough journey, I might have felt myself to be the victim of a hellish experience.

Also, I had to match myself to the pace of the group and the dictates of the land. To adjust my rhythm was to experience my essence in harmony with a rugged environment. I could not make it easier, nor could I do it "my way." The way of the land had authority: dusk brought out the predators. Yet, as the sights became ever more wondrous, our trek through the bush took on magical qualities.

Like my accepting the travails of our trek, accepting the challenge to awaken means making necessary attitude adjustments and willingly facing hardship. We must endeavor to do these things without feeling like a victim. In the process of awakening from perfectionism, we seek to match the rhythm of Essence, speeding up or slowing down when necessary, as we welcome the rugged adventures of a wondrous journey.

Following One's Own Path

There is no one true Way, because the Way for each person is distinct. Each individual's path is illuminated by Inner Guidance. We must heed our guidance and trust it, especially if the path we're being shown looks different from the paths of others. It is a mistake to compare ourselves to others; to do so invites the Perfectionist's self-inflation or -deflation. What's more, we can never know the challenges faced by another.

Look at another person's life for learning and inspiration, not in order to build yourself up or put yourself down. When you notice self-mastery, observe that individual with the intention of being uplifted in some way. If you begin to judge yourself on the basis of another's accomplishments or seeming happiness, stop yourself and request guidance.

HOW DO YOU COMPARE YOURSELF TO OTHERS?
IN DOING THIS, WHAT ARE YOU TRYING TO PROVE?

Open Your Heart to Yourself

As I discussed in Chapter Three, Inner Guidance can be accessed in many ways. Use the system of your choice to tap into your wisdom source, and keep your process of awakening fresh and alive. Continual vigilance is important. If, in your awakening process, the Perfectionist is employed to serve Essence, all will be well. But if the Perfectionist retains control, it will cause the kind of trouble with which you are already familiar.

My teacher once told me that, to receive Inner Guidance, all I really had to do was open my heart. I was instructed to meditate on this every day. My "good girl" was fierce then, so every day I practiced ripping open my heart. I struggled intensely, in my jackhammer style, and got nowhere. But I persevered, believing that my commitment would see me through.

Sometimes I would feel my heart begin to open, and I'd get overly eager and push it. This, of course, shut my heart up tightly again. My teacher told me I was trying too hard. He said that I needed to be softer with my heart and allow it to open, without trying to force it. I had no grasp of this allowing business. I thought, *You take control or you don't.*

One day, during my meditation, I saw (in my mind's eye) my heart open like a crack in a wall. A warm light emanated from the crack. Then I saw a frightened, animal-like creature clutching with its hands, feet, and tail to the pieces of my heart. It behaved as if it would die if my heart opened. My guidance told me to close my heart again and to promise this little creature that I would no longer try to force it open.

After my heart was securely closed, I imagined myself taking the frightened thing down from my heart and letting it rest on the ground while I soothed its sobs and shivers. I sensed that this was the most frightened and vulnerable part of me (the part that my Perfectionist had considered weak), and that my job was to make it feel safe, for it was the gatekeeper of my heart.

Now I understood that it was the fear of vulnerability, behind my Arrogance and my Greed for emotional truth, that was causing my heart's gatekeeper to fear Self-Destruction. I realized that I had always believed my heart couldn't open because I was a bad person.

My meditative experience with that part of myself was a great relief to me. I was happy to know that I was not hard and bad, just frightened. Every day for two weeks, I looked in to see how my little gatekeeper creature was doing. I felt tenderness toward it, and enjoyed giving it comfort. My attitude about myself and what I was doing began to change. I realized that I had needed to open my heart to the weakest part of myself as my first step.

About two weeks later, in meditation, I saw my new friend sitting with me in the first row of a movie theater, in front of a big, heart-shaped, silver screen. We had our arms around each other and were sharing popcorn, both happily anticipating the opening of my heart. I felt a rush of warmth and light permeate me as my heart completely opened. After that, I knew the difference between forcing and allowing.

I was reminded of that experience again just today, many years and meditations later, because I had to learn it again. When my "good girl" gets stuck trying to do the right thing, I'm caught in my Perfectionist's push again and have to learn anew how to accept and allow myself. My Perfectionist also thinks I should know this one by now, but the truth is, I will be relearning it for the rest of my life. So be it.

If you can open your heart to the weakest, most frightened or vulnerable part of yourself, your Perfectionist will lose power. It's only being sustained by a lack of self-acceptance.

WHAT IS THE WEAKEST PART OF YOU?
PRACTICE OPENING YOUR HEART TO IT.

Accepting Loss

Recovery from perfectionism is sometimes accompanied by feelings of loss. When we see how the freedom gained from following Inner Guidance contrasts with the pain of the past, we may feel the need to grieve for lost time and missed opportunities. Sometimes there is the feeling of a loss of personality, as the highs and lows of our experiences level out. We may miss the familiar edge, may fear becoming too boring as the eccentricities of the false self fade away.

I had always known myself as intense, moody, or feisty. In groups, I struggled openly or caused some kind of controversy. But the more I softened my perfectionism and followed Inner Guidance, the more I mellowed out, until in time I had considerably less to say. I was no longer the standout in groups. It seemed as if I no longer knew myself, and that was a little unnerving. A statement in the Alanon twelve-step program refers to this disorientation: "What's wrong? Nothing's wrong, that's what's wrong."

These feelings are natural. They usually mean that we are on a bridge between the old and the new ways of being. We are no longer who we used to be. We may have lost some of our old identity, fantasies, and relationships. A new sense of purpose and the people who will share it with us are not yet fully within view.

If we are accustomed to confusing anxiety with aliveness, anger with power, and obsession with love and passion, this will be a time of reorganizing priorities. It is natural for us to wish to return to the old familiar ways of being, but they don't fit anymore. All we need do during this time is keep feeling, so that our feelings can catch up with our changes. Soon the struggle will seem like an exciting journey, and the new way of being will start to take on a feeling of comfort.

LET YOURSELF FEEL YOUR LOSSES.

Begin Where You Are

The Perfectionist doesn't know how to take small steps. It condemns the place where it is, and strives to be higher, faster, slimmer, better. Sheila inherited enough money to support herself for several years. When her money started running out, she wanted to get a mid-level job because she needed to earn enough to support her lifestyle. However, she had neither the training nor the confidence to apply.

Sheila was unwilling to get an entry-level position, because it would not support her accustomed lifestyle. In the time she spent resisting the facts, she could have started at an entry-level position and moved up to mid-level. She waited until her money was gone and she had to live on credit cards before she realized that she couldn't skip the first step.

It is necessary to come down from grandiosity (the Perfectionist) and up from self-doubt (Helpless) into the real self. The challenge is to let the real self be good enough. There is immense freedom in the realization that it is okay to be exactly the way you are. The Perfectionist believes that some of the people in the world are jerks, weak, or crazy and some of the people in the world are perfect. Actually, everyone is part jerk, part weak, and part crazy. And that is the perfect setup, because when you don't have to change yourself, then it becomes possible for change to happen.

WHERE ARE YOU TRYING TO GET AHEAD OF YOURSELF?

The Nature of Change

Like prevailing winds or the course of a river, change is determined by natural forces. Most of life's changes are beyond our conscious control; we can at best only surrender to them and flow with them. If we can maintain an attitude of openness to whatever changes may come, life will support us in adjusting to those shifts.

Positive changes cannot be forced. The attitude of demand or self-rejection "pushes the river": *In order to be acceptable, I have to change.* This attitude leaves no opening for Inner Guidance to be engaged and natural order to have its way. The condition of self-acceptance allows us to "go with the flow": *I want to give this change to myself.*

Even when we are open to change, and even when Inner Guidance is in charge, certain parts of the psyche will fight life's transitions. All change involves opposing forces. The Perfectionist wants only the changes that it can control, and it wants them yesterday. Helpless wants only the "nice" changes that come from someone else's efforts. Together, these two parts of the psyche resist or push for change, and in so doing block life's flow. It is unrealistic to try to eliminate their influence. Rather, our rate of change has to accommodate the tension of these opposites.

Lasting change is preceded by successive levels of learning. The Perfectionist is stuck on the level of the intellect. It thinks that, once the mind has grasped something, change should immediately follow: *You already know about that. Why don't you do it?* Helpless is stuck on the emotional level: *I don't feel like it.* Knowing needs to be processed through the mind, emotions, body, and spirit before it can bring about lasting change.

Marilyn struggled for several years to end a destructive relationship with a man who wouldn't marry her. Charles stayed out nights drinking, and punched the walls when Marilyn complained. She would slingshot in and out of the relationship, because each time she left she couldn't sustain the change. At the start of our work, I asked Marilyn to stop pushing herself to leave and to, instead, open herself to the natural flow of change. Her process needed to take her through enough levels to allow the change to hold.

At her current level, Marilyn viewed the end of her relationship as a loss of love that she must endure. Life can't flow through that kind of thinking, which was pushing away something she needed (love) and offering nothing to replace it. Marilyn needed to view the end of the relationship as something she wanted to give herself. Attention on what is wanted is more open to flow than attention on what one is giving up. She also needed to remember what she wanted (to be married and treated well) in real terms, not fantasy terms.

Receiving support creates more flow, and Marilyn needed support to sustain her in her struggle. She needed books, therapy, and twelve-step meetings, but not advice from family or friends. Her belief that she wasn't good enough to be treated well was another impediment to the flow of change. She couldn't leave destructive love until she opened to receive something better.

Marilyn needed to begin where she was. Her Helpless part said, *I can't bear to lose him.* Her Perfectionist said, *You must leave him now.* This conflict blocked Marilyn's readiness. Learning that she didn't have to leave until she was ready relieved the pressure, and removed another obstacle that had blocked the flow of change.

Marilyn then had the time and freedom to engage her Inner Guidance, which flows in by itself when we remove the interference. Her guidance, combined with outer support, gradually shifted the balance between Marilyn's immediate fear of loss and her allegiance to what she really wanted. Within six months, she had passed through enough levels of learning to leave Charles—without the needless suffering that comes from trying to force or resist change. She let go of the connection because it was no longer in keeping with her relationship with herself.

Within the next eighteen months, after one brief "bridging" relationship, Marilyn met her husband-to-be. The relationship is not perfect, but it is one of genuine caring and respect—a reflection of her increased self-appreciation. Marilyn has found new fulfillment in love because she has learned to work with, not against, the nature of change.

NOTICE WHERE YOU PUSH CHANGE,
AND WHERE YOU RESIST IT.

Mindfulness

The first step in identifying the Perfectionist and distinguishing it from Inner Guidance is mindfulness. Waking up to the Perfectionist is like discovering a lifelong conspiracy that's been going on in your head. As much as we fear conspiracies, we don't want to believe in them. The will to disbelieve, combined with the Perfectionist's wish to remain hidden, adds up to a formidable challenge. Meeting a challenge of this scope requires that our full attention be directed into self-observation.

The task for students of Inner Guidance is to see the Perfectionist in action by noticing its attempts to inflate or deflate self-esteem. But we cannot set the Perfectionist to find the Perfectionist. So, in addition to observing oneself, one needs to ask, "Who's doing the looking?"

Whenever we are able to observe the Perfectionist without judgment, we know that the real self is doing the looking. But if we catch ourselves trying to prove, "I'm good/bad," or "they're good/bad," it is the Perfectionist that's doing the looking. The work then is to simply notice oneself—*What am I doing?*—like a scientist or a journalist, gathering data from a neutral, somewhat detached and skeptical position. Inner Guidance will do the rest.

Trying to move into self-correction prematurely, before learning mindfulness, causes a loss of both neutrality and curiosity, and with these is lost the connection to Inner Guidance. To attempt to correct at this stage is to attempt too much. The work is not to correct, but to be curious and to notice, without judgment. Correction will come later, through Inner Guidance.

WHEN YOU ARE OBSERVING YOURSELF,
WHO IS DOING THE LOOKING?

Suffering

One of the hardest truths for me to accept has been that suffering is a necessary part of life. It comes and goes like a force of nature, and cannot be controlled. However, allowing ourselves to follow perfectionism leads to unnecessary suffering.

The Perfectionist's belief that suffering is wrong only increases our suffering. According to the Perfectionist, we are wrong if we suffer, the world is wrong because there is suffering in it, life is wrong because it brings suffering, and God is wrong for allowing suffering. But trying to run away from suffering causes it to chase you. If you say to suffering, *Oh no, not you again—go away!* the pain just gets worse.

My client Janice fought an oncoming depression. She tried to turn her negative thoughts into positive thinking. My own efforts to help keep her out of depression were failing. I felt a sense of futility, and wondered if that was what she was feeling.

I asked Janice if she felt her struggle was futile. "Yes," was her reply. I suggested that she just let herself feel her depression and not try to resist it. Maybe her Inner Guidance would begin to lift her, and she wouldn't have to use so much energy trying to uplift herself.

That perspective moved Janice into relief. As long as she had judged her pain as wrong, and wouldn't let herself feel it, she had remained stuck. When she allowed herself to feel it, her Inner Guidance gave her some associated memories from the past, which were followed by the emotional release of crying. Janice then reached a deeper understanding of herself that would not have come had she continued to avoid her suffering. The avoidance had increased and prolonged her suffering unnecessarily, and had delayed the healing experience that she needed.

The Perfectionist's value judgments can be the very obstacles that prevent the growth it says it wants. It has the power and intelligence to grow, but it lacks awareness—of its limitations, of the human within, of the fact that it lacks awareness.

Suffering, instead of being seen as wrong, can serve as a signal to pay attention—a reminder to ask for its message instead of recoiling from it. Curiosity activates Inner Guidance. Staying open and receptive in the presence of suffering, instead of trying to push it away, can reveal whether we need to do something or simply let the pain pass through. Instead of trying to avoid suffering, change your relationship to it.

IS THERE SOME PAIN THAT YOU ARE AVOIDING?
WHAT WOULD HAPPEN IF YOU LET YOURSELF FEEL IT?

Self-Talk

In your search for the Perfectionist, I suggest that you pay particular attention to the different voices in your mind. Listen to what they say. Is there a voice that calls you stupid? That says you are slow, selfish, worthless? Do you hear demands such as, *Just do it—hurry up!* and *Now look what you've done*? Do you hear invectives such as, *You can't do that—you're wasting time!* or *You always . . .* or *You never . . .* ? Does that voice dwell in the past and predict the future? *It's always going to be like it was—or worse.* Noticing self-talk or the way you talk to other people will help you pinpoint how the Perfectionist affects you and your relationships.

It is important not to prematurely correct your negative self-talk with positive self-talk. Trying to replace negative thoughts with positive just clogs the Inner Guidance channel and wastes more energy. Remember: curiosity and neutral self-observation invite Inner Guidance. Balance will start to be restored with increased awareness of the effects of negative self-talk. Then the next step will be to stop listening to self-talk and start listening for Inner Guidance.

NOTICE HOW YOU SPEAK TO YOURSELF.

Body Signals

Thoughts and self-talk affect emotions and moods. Emotions and moods are accompanied by physical sensations that, when identified and interpreted, help to clarify Inner Guidance. When we say, "I feel angry/ nervous/pressured/scared/happy," there is a corresponding sensation. We might feel a hot face, a sinking feeling, a weight on the shoulders, a knot in the stomach, a fullness in the chest. When we don't know what we think and feel, these body sensations can tell us. They are signals from Inner Guidance.

The body feelings that accompany perfectionism are different from those that come from Essence, but it takes an inquiry to clearly distinguish them. When we feel pressure, anger, or any other discomfort, and we make no inquiry, we're inclined to automatically do something quick to relieve the discomfort. Though this choice may work for the moment, it causes unwanted future consequences.

Yet, if we give some time and attention to the body sensations, they have messages to reveal to us. Asking the sensations to reveal more, instead of making quick assumptions about what's causing our discomfort, will summon the experience of our Inner Guidance. Insights can then enter the mind, like gifts from a mysterious source.

Intuition may come as a hunch, an "Aha!" or a fresh idea. In this way, we may discover that the source of the pressure is an unrealistic expectation or an exaggerated response to a situation—both of which are the work of the wily Perfectionist. Our inquiry relieves the discomfort by detecting any misunderstanding, and restores well-being by strengthening the connection to Inner Guidance.

WHEN YOU PAY ATTENTION TO YOUR BODY'S
SIGNALS, WHAT DO THEY TELL YOU?

Self-Knowledge

The clarity of Inner Guidance is largely dependent upon self-knowledge, which means to know oneself. We all have identities, or formed ideas of ourselves, that exclude factors we don't yet know. To better know ourselves means to venture cautiously into the unknown, because this inquiry will threaten the Perfectionist. The way needs to be made safe. Certain misconceptions about the unknown cause us to fear it and avoid it. But when we back away from self-exploration, we miss the treasures that lie in the hidden places of our psyche.

WHERE IN YOUR OWN PSYCHE
DO YOU STILL FEAR TO VENTURE?

The Dark Side

The dark side or shadow is often considered to be the hidden "bad parts" of the psyche. Unfortunately, that perception tends to discourage any looking beneath the surface. In actual fact, the dark side is simply the part of us that we don't yet know, and because it is unknown it is often misunderstood.

If a personality in formation gets mirrored in such a way that a trait is criticized or goes unnoticed, that trait gets buried in the dark side. It stays there dormant, but builds up pressure because it has a natural need to come up and be acknowledged. If the trait is forced to stay down, it starts to gain potency, and it may fuel addictions until we set it free. This trait is not always a negative one; it may be an asset that was met with disapproval.

Mary thought she was a bad person. She was afraid to look at her dark side, for fear that she would find out just how horrible she was. She assumed that what she didn't know about herself was even worse than what she did know. But, as she and I gently approached the unknown parts of her, she was surprised to discover strengths and talents. Mary's positive traits had not been mirrored by the important people in her life, so she had never learned that she had them.

To protect self-esteem and avoid further injury, the Perfectionist drives our disliked and unnoticed parts into hiding. It then becomes a lifelong sentry, devoted to keeping these elements hidden away like a rejected twin locked in the attic.

Bringing our secret traits out of hiding and making peace with them is the key to the fulfillment that eludes us. The parts of ourselves that we don't want to meet are the very ones we most need. Think of your incomplete self-concept as the tip of an iceberg, and the complete you as the entire iceberg. It might be good to consider going down under the surface to meet the rest of yourself.

WHAT HIDDEN PARTS OF YOURSELF ARE WAITING TO BE
BROUGHT UP OUT OF THE DARKNESS AND INTO THE LIGHT?

Even Jerks Can Do Good Work

The word "jerk" is an offensive put-down, yet isn't it what we secretly call ourselves, along with other disparaging names? Haven't we heard ourselves refer to others by that term? At the height of my struggle, my teacher told me, "Cynthia, no matter how hard you try to perfect yourself, you're still going to be a jerk. But that's okay. I'm a jerk too, and even jerks can do good work." After the initial shock wore off, I found that these words had pierced a hole in my self-importance. And, like time-released wisdom, they continue to take me off the big hook of having to prove myself.

I have occasionally upset people by telling them that I am part jerk. Their response has been, "Don't think that about yourself. You are not a jerk!" in a tone that implied, "You're a jerk to think you're a jerk." Contrary to what they thought, I was not criticizing myself. I was freeing myself. Once we know that everyone is part jerk and part crazy, we don't have to worry and hide anymore. If we want to clear the way for our sense of purpose, we perfectionists have to get really honest with ourselves in this way. That's how we can gain the self-knowledge and self-acceptance that precedes accomplishment.

IN WHAT AREAS CAN YOU OWN UP TO BEING A JERK?
CAN YOU LOVE YOURSELF ANYWAY?

9

Coming Into the Moment

Inner Guidance happens in the moment. The Perfectionist avoids the moment, because to it the moment feels too hot, too empty, or too close for comfort. It prefers the buffer zone of the past or future. Yet, it controls the moment—by pulling you out of it.

Trying to stay in the moment often means feeling the Perfectionist breathing down your neck, saying, *That bad thing that happened in the past is about to happen again.* Your fear takes you out of the moment, and another opportunity to experience something new is missed.

Being in the moment means attuning your awareness to this breath, this heartbeat, this single event. I invite you to notice and feel whatever is right here, right now. Endure the Perfectionist's harangue about wasting time. Come into the moment—"switch on."

A Choice Made by Default

Every week Julie spoke rapidly, as if trying to stay ahead of something, about how much she hated her job and her relationship. She would then shift to describing her optimistic plans for the future. I asked her if she had any ideas about how to bridge the life she hated to the life she wanted. She began speaking even more rapidly, searching for the right answers while looking at me for approval. I said I didn't know the answers, but that I'd bet she did if she would slow down a little to listen for them. Julie burst into tears—the tears she had been trying to avoid with her fast talking and forced optimism. The tears cleared the way for her wisdom.

The choices we make in each moment determine our future. Avoiding the moment is a choice made by default, and this choice causes a discrepancy between the life we plan and the life we live. When our idea of ourself doesn't match our behavior, and the result we get continually fails to match the result we want, we have not yet come into the moment.

The path from where you are to where you want to go is found in the heat of the moment. To stay in the moment, try affirming something like the following: *The bad thing that happened in the past may not happen in the future if I can hold myself steady in the here and now, request guidance, and then stay put, ignoring the Perfectionist's diversions, until the guidance arrives.*

PRACTICE COMING INTO THE MOMENT,
ALONE AND WITH ANOTHER PERSON.

Balance and the Law of Cause and Effect

No matter how sincere one's intentions or how great one's responsibilities, when the body or mind loses enough of its balance, the show will stop. This will happen through some kind of illness, breakdown, addictive behavior, or personal revolt. It is a manifestation of the law of cause and effect. I have personally experienced this law in action a number of times, when I let my Perfectionist push me too far or when life turned left and I continued straight ahead in allegiance to my Perfectionist. I have been thrashed, bashed, slapped down, slam dunked, and planted firmly in my bed.

I used to think of these experiences as punishment, injustice, or betrayals. Now I think of them as refresher courses in the law of cause and effect. I thought my responsibilities or my noble causes should make me exempt from this law, but I found out that there are no special dispensations. If I get too far out of balance, I will be stopped. And then I will have to do whatever is necessary to regain my balance. The law of cause and effect doesn't care if I can't afford to take time off work.

My latest attempt to negotiate with the law of cause and effect has been the writing of this book. Staying in balance requires that my process be insufferably slow, which drives my Perfectionist crazy. So I must laugh in the face of my Perfectionist, saying, *Hah! You can't pressure me to speed up. I will not let you write this book, no matter how badly you want to!*

I must also surrender to the realization that my Perfectionist intrudes itself into my writing. I can't have been run by perfectionism my whole life and expect it to go away now that I'm writing a book about it. So I am learning to live in relative balance with my Perfectionist, too. And that is indeed possible, now that I know that I have the guidance of a greater authority within me.

My study of the reemergence of the mind-body approach to medicine gives support and meaning to my personal struggle. We, as individuals, can be strengthened to resist the Perfectionist when it opposes our attempts to restore ourselves to balance.

In the process of regaining balance, some fallow time may be necessary. It is important to hold the right attitude, and not to sink into the depression that can result from reduced activity. Stillness may be reminiscent of past collapses, but this time the stillness is contributing to a return to balance and a restoration of the spirit. You are crossing a threshold: leaving behind the Perfectionist's push and your resulting depletion, and advancing to a place where you can allow yourself to receive support from Essence. Your attitude—the meaning and reverence that you give to this crossing—can sustain you through any accompanying depression.

*WHERE IN YOUR LIFE ARE YOU ATTEMPTING TO IGNORE
THE LAW OF CAUSE AND EFFECT BY GETTING OUT OF BALANCE?*

Work, Study, Rest, and Play

Balance in the areas of work, study, rest, and play is essential. Resistance to this balance is the Backslide. The Perfectionist will do anything to prevent balance, because balance is the antidote to perfectionism. If you lean toward inactivity, create balance by adding activity and movement. If you overwork your mind, balance that with a mindless activity or with just plain rest.

Work

Lack of work can be as debilitating as overwork. Feeling unproductive dims the life force and is fertile ground for Helpless. Once one falls into Helpless, it is hard to get started again. Until Inner Guidance is known, the Perfectionist attempts another rescue. It responds like a pit bull that won't let go, driving Helpless over the edge of perfectionism and back into helplessness again. Work isn't just about earning money. One needs to feel vital, and vitality is lost in over- or underproduction.

Study

The Perfectionist says that knowledge should be inherent, that beginners are failures. It avoids feelings of frustration by making up excuses for us not to learn new things: *If I can't be good at it, I don't want to do it at all.* Yet, for balance, study needs to take its place with the rest of our life activities. It is good to be a student of something all through life. I find that life itself is my teacher; every day my lessons take new forms. Learning to recover from my perfectionism is one of those forms.

You can be a student of your own recovery process. Once you decide to give up striving to be perfect, your process takes on a life force of its own. We don't have to know how it works, but we can study it as we go. I learn much about perfectionism recovery from witnessing my clients' self-discoveries.

Rest

Rest takes different forms for different people. For some, it means sleeping or just lying in bed. Others may take their rest by reading or gardening or listening to music. Getting out and exercising makes some people feel rested, while others unwind by spending time with animals. Some are rested by immersing themselves in nature and in wilderness experiences. Find out what rests you, and balance that with your work, study, and play.

Play

Play is every bit as essential as work. The Perfectionist loathes fun: it's not serious or productive enough. But fun is very productive, for we can't operate effectively without it. Perhaps that's why Plato said, "Life must be lived as play."

If you are undermotivated in your work, look for a deficit of fun in your life. Such a deficit causes the inner child to go on strike. A fierce perfectionist may obscure our experience of the inner child, but it is still there—made miserable by neglect. No matter how old we become, this child never grows up. Our inner child has our sense of wonder, our inspiration and motivation, and the power to pull the plug on other endeavors when it's been too long since we let it out to play.

Like rest, play also takes many forms. We may travel, keep a collection, dress up for a special event, engage in a board game with friends, or spend time doing home decorating. Anything recreational that delights us and gives us pleasure qualifies as play.

*CONSIDER THE ACTIVITIES OF WORK, STUDY, REST, AND PLAY.
IS YOUR LIFE OUT OF BALANCE IN ANY OF THESE AREAS?*

Accepting Support

Contrary to the Perfectionist's idea of strength, receiving support is not a sign of weakness, it is a universal need. When it comes to this need, you and I are no exception. We don't get any points for doing things all by ourselves. Nor are there any intimate relationships that involve giving without receiving.

I have my own Support Hall of Fame, in which the most honored inductee is a certain dear friend. Connie came over one evening and found me lying in misery on the living room floor.

"Do you have Lioness Lethargy?" she asked. (Connie is good at coming up with creative terminology for various emotional states.)

"Yes," I whined. "I want to go to bed, but I can't wash my face and brush my teeth."

Connie disappeared, and reappeared with a bowl of warm water, a face cloth, and my toothbrush. Right there on the floor, she washed my face and brushed my teeth.

Not all support from friends can qualify for the Support Hall of Fame, yet support of some kind is essential in neutralizing the Perfectionist. Not only can we gratefully accept support from others, but we can be generous with our own support, as well. Since perfectionism continually seeks new ways to remain in control, there's nothing like receiving perpetual support from like-minded others to soften its hold.

Faith in external support systems, when combined with faith in internal resources, maximizes the forces of nature to promote health and well-being. That's why the support of other recovering perfectionists—others who are in the process of rediscovering their essence—is so precious.

> *WHEN WAS THE LAST TIME YOU ACCEPTED SUPPORT?*
> *WHEN WAS THE LAST TIME YOU ASKED FOR IT?*
> *WHEN WAS THE LAST TIME YOU PUSHED IT AWAY?*

Humor—the Saving Grace

The Perfectionist has no sense of humor. It sees only our flaws and failings. To expose these failings is to show weakness, and to laugh at them is unthinkable. I don't encourage self-negating put-down humor. But I do suggest that you learn to laugh at the way you build yourself up or put yourself down.

My friend John had some know-it-all tendencies, of which he was well aware. Whenever he caught himself on his soapbox, he would abruptly end his speech by sardonically quoting himself: "Jonathan Harris Randle the Third, Ph.D." (He did not have a III after his name, nor did he have a Ph.D.). I loved it. It made me feel closer to John, and also made him feel closer to himself. This kind of humor includes an element of confession.

Now that I am recovering from perfectionism, I can laugh at myself much more than I ever could before. Those areas in which I cannot laugh at myself remain under the Perfectionist's control, and in those areas I know that I am still too self-rejecting.

> *NOTICE WHERE YOU CAN LAUGH AT YOURSELF,*
> *AND WHERE YOU CANNOT.*
> *STRETCH TO "POKE A LITTLE FUN" AT YOURSELF.*

The Art of Whining

When you hear yourself childishly whining, take the opportunity to explore it and gain some valuable self-knowledge. Inside of every whine, there is a critical but forbidden need. This need can be discovered if we take an interest in our own whining.

A whine sounds like a balloon when you let a little of the air out. The air in the balloon is under pressure. If you let the air out all at once, the balloon flies around the room. A whine reveals a forbidden need that is under a lot of pressure. If we encourage the whine, we learn about the need, and can then do something to relieve the pressure.

My friend John and I used to play a game that started spontaneously after we saw the movie *What About Bob?* with Bill Murray. In the movie, Bill Murray's character seeks psychotherapy from Richard Dreyfuss's character. He is in great need, and in complete acceptance of his neediness. He says repeatedly, "I need." I think most of us would agree that to need all the time is an obnoxious trait. But can't we welcome a little of this needy quality in order to learn a lot?

When John or I start to whine, the other one hears it as a signal to explore the buried need. When John whines, I ask, "Do you need?" He says, "Yes." I ask, "Do you know what you need?" He says, "No, but I sure can feel it." Then we explore together. "Is it this? Is it that? What does it look like? What does it feel like? Is it old? Is it new?" The child in John can't get right to his need because, at some point in his life, the need was forbidden.

When we use humor, and offer another's whining child a warm reception, an unmet need is soon revealed. Then its pressure can be relieved; sometimes the very revealing of the need is all it takes to do this. This doesn't mean, however, that once a need is known, one has to fill it for the other. Maybe I can, maybe I can't; maybe he can, maybe he can't. But certainly nobody can, until we know what it is.

FIND A FRIEND WHO WILL PRACTICE WHINING WITH YOU.

The Benefits of Tears

The Perfectionist dismisses Aristotle's two-thousand-year-old claim that crying "cleanses the mind," because the Perfectionist disapproves of crying. It regards tears as weak, self-indulgent, and self-pitying. At the very least, it thinks, *Crying will ruin my makeup.*

I like what Dr. Clarissa Pinkola Estés says in her book *Women Who Run With the Wolves*: "Tears are a river that take you somewhere. Weeping creates a river around the boat that carries your soul-life. Tears lift your boat off the rocks, off dry ground, carrying it down river to someplace new, someplace better."

Crying is an integral part of my perfectionism recovery process. Generally speaking, the less I cry, the more physically ill I feel. My Perfectionist taught me to somatize my emotions. I suppress them, they get stuck in my body, and they then result in depression and physical pain. When I cry, providing I am in relative balance and self-care, my depression lifts, my pain subsides, and I soon feel buoyant. (Please note that, when I encourage crying, I am not referring to Helpless's crocodile tears.)

We can't force ourselves to cry. Even if we could, this would be as counterproductive as holding tears in. What we can do is gradually change our attitude toward crying, by welcoming the release of tears. As a child, I was afraid to cry in front of my mother. Now, when my Perfectionist is active, my inner child is afraid to cry in front of me. But that is something I intend to change.

HOW DO YOU FEEL ABOUT YOURSELF WHEN YOU CRY?

Becoming Your Own Fair Witness

One practice that aids mindfulness is to call the Perfectionist "it." When clients say, "I'm so mad at myself!" I suggest that they say instead, "*It* is mad at me." This has two beneficial effects. For one thing, to be able to observe the Perfectionist it is necessary to separate from it. Secondly, when we say, "It is mad at me," we also get in touch with the parts of ourselves that are *not* angry at us. One such part I have termed the fair witness.

The fair witness is a natural resource that can be found (even though it may be dormant) inside every person. Our own curiosity activates this fair witness, which we can call upon to relieve pressure, reduce anxiety, increase safety, engage our Inner Guidance, and ultimately break the Perfectionist's obsessive control.

The first time I remember learning the value of the fair witness was during a conflict in a therapy class. One student said she felt victimized by her neighbors and was certain she had no part in the problem. In the name of "helpful feedback," we ganged up on this student. My Perfectionist had deduced her blind spot, and found her to be entirely too rigid. I was "the pot calling the kettle black." The other students and I tried to push some sense into her (a favorite technique of the Perfectionist). It didn't matter if our advice was right, because our approach was wrong. The harder we pushed, the more she shut down.

The instructor took a different approach. He became gently curious—even fascinated—about the experience this student was having with the rest of the class. Implicit in his communication was, "You don't have to agree with them. But I wonder what is happening here?" The student softened under the instructor's unprejudiced interest in her.

I watched as he made her feel safe enough to reveal herself to him and to reassess her own position. I've since learned that the power of impartial curiosity works just as well when we apply it to ourselves. We cannot open to learning in the presence of the Perfectionist's cold-blooded scrutiny, but we can open in the presence of a fair witness.

WATCH YOURSELF WITH FASCINATION.

Redirecting Your Attention

I often hear clients say, "I have to get rid of that," in reference to something they don't like about themselves. But it is a natural law that we can't get rid of anything. The harder we try to rid ourselves of something (weight, emotions, addictions, perfectionism), the more the thing will hold on for dear life.

Rejection of a characteristic just doesn't work. To be against something has no power; the key is to be for something else. An unwanted trait can be diminished by redirecting attention to a preferred one. One can weaken the characteristic by politely refusing to give it energy, and diverting that energy toward a substitute trait.

There is a big difference between polite refusal and avoidance. Calm refusal of the Perfectionist's demands has authority and autonomy, while avoidance lacks both. To avoid is to hide passively, hoping not to get caught. Such avoidance actually feeds the Perfectionist.

To redirect your attention from the Perfectionist is to say, *I see you, I hear you, and I choose not to follow you.* Don't try to change its mind, and don't merely oppose it. Ask for guidance: *Does any other part of me have a different perspective?* This stance will activate Inner Guidance and reduce the power of the Perfectionist.

PRACTICE REFUSING ALL OF THE PERFECTIONIST'S DEMANDS, AS YOU REDIRECT YOUR ATTENTION TO INNER GUIDANCE.

Human Needs

As we have seen, our attempts to ignore our own needs, fears, and weaknesses or to make them go away don't work. Yet, the preoccupation with needs, fears, and weaknesses prevents us from fully living. Here, too, we need to achieve a balance. The middle way lies somewhere between denial and wallowing.

If it is not possible to change a need, it is still possible to change one's relationship to it. But first, the basic needs must be known. Universal human needs include:

- Physical nourishment: food, warmth, comfort, safety
- Emotional nourishment: love, attention, affection, acceptance, contact
- Mental nourishment: not just believing what one is taught or told, but forming an understanding of the self and the world through direct personal inquiry
- Spiritual nourishment: a sense of purpose, belonging, participation, and contribution

These needs are nonnegotiable; we cannot achieve fulfillment without them. Injuries from the past in any of these areas cause fear and weakness. If we do not attend to the injuries, they submerge themselves and erupt as seemingly disconnected addictions or complexes, which then demand even more time and attention just to unravel them back to the original need. Thus it is best for us to relinquish self-blame (since we are all subject to these needs and injuries), accept responsibility for overcoming our addictions, and address the original unmet needs through self-care.

DO YOU KNOW ALL OF YOUR NEEDS? DO YOU WANT TO?

Self-Care

I have tried all my life to be a low-maintenance woman, a trouper, ready in an instant for anything. My childhood caused me to not want to be a bother to anyone. It was part of my need to be strong and self-sufficient, or (more accurately) not weak and not needy. The truth is that, from the beginning of my life, I was always a little sickly. This was made worse by the fact that I didn't learn how to take care of myself.

As I grew older, instead of taking care of my real needs, I willed myself to be stronger than I was. Self-care seemed an indulgent waste of time and effort. My Helpless part just didn't feel up to doing it, while My Perfectionist thought I shouldn't need it. Each of these attitudes contributed to my chronic illness.

My avoidance of minimal self-care caused a condition that required endless self-care—another manifestation of the law of cause and effect. If we dig ourselves into a deep hole, we have to dig out just to break even.

Self-nurturance, in the big picture, is a balance of work, study, rest, and play. Besides ensuring that our daily life gives us enough sleep, exercise, nutrition, and preventative medical care, we must balance the outer world with our inner life—"their needs" with our own.

REVEL IN SELF-CARE.

Self-Discipline

The Perfectionist's version of self-discipline is a harsh taskmaster that arises from self-doubt and from mistrust of human nature. Yet the root meaning of self-discipline is "to become a disciple of the self." This kind of self-discipline activates Inner Guidance, and gives endeavors a devotional quality. Devotional self-discipline is a natural extension of opening your heart to yourself. This approach enables disbelievers to become self-believers and life-believers.

My ambition wanted to begin writing this book years before I was ready, but ambition was insufficient motivation. I had to believe in myself as well. So I entered a period of preparation and waited for my guidance to prompt me to begin. My waiting had to be balanced with the knowledge that the Perfectionist's "self-discipline" can evaporate a vision by simultaneously saying *Just do it* while it is weakening our belief that we can do it. It then punishes us for not doing it.

At some point I recognized that I might be waiting too long, and that I needed some support to begin. I went to a writing workshop, where I received inspiration and practical advice. Author Tom Robbins told a story about waiting for his muse. He thought it would be really funny if, while he waited at the lake for his muse to show up, it was waiting for him at his desk. He decided to show up at his desk every day so his muse would know where to find him. I liked his light approach to self-discipline, and took some of it away with me.

WHAT IS YOUR RELATIONSHIP TO SELF-DISCIPLINE?
BECOME A DISCIPLE OF YOURSELF.

Breaking Rules

To be self-governing, we need the authority to say no to the Perfectionist. Devotional self-discipline must include the ability to break rules. The right use of mindfulness, listening to self-talk, exploring body signals, and the identification of specific types of perfectionism will reveal the rules that need to be broken.

Once we learn what these rules are, we need to be judicious, for breaking rules indiscriminately can be self-destructive. The prudent use of rule breaking will defuse the Perfectionist's control and serve to further our autonomy.

Whenever we break one of the Perfectionist's rules, it attempts to regain control through a backlash of guilt, self-criticism, or fear of retribution. There is a backlash for every broken rule, and we must learn how to weather it. We can begin with the breaking of minor rules, and practice riding out small storms. Constructive refusal of the Perfectionist's demands will make us more effective in our endeavors, which will encourage us to go for more.

The backlashes decrease in proportion to our increasing autonomy. Break a given rule by reversing it into a form that extends trust, relieves pressure, and invites freedom. "Work now, rest later" becomes "Rest now, work later." "Don't cry" becomes "Cry all you want to." "Don't be ordinary" becomes "Dare to be ordinary." "Don't make mistakes" becomes "Dare to make mistakes." "Stop whining" becomes "Whining is encouraged."

THINK ABOUT THE RULES THAT YOU LIVE BY.
WHICH ONES WOULD YOU LIKE TO BREAK?

Beginning Again

In any new growth process, there is a honeymoon period. Thereafter, the process invariably loses some of its luster. This is the point at which the Backslide attempts to reclaim whatever gains the individual has made. Since this is to be expected, precautions can be taken. To defuse the Perfectionist and engage Inner Guidance will require learning how to begin again. We need to be prepared to outlast the Perfectionist's attempts to regain control. And it will regain control, over and over again. Yet we will transcend our perfectionism and achieve success by starting over each time the Perfectionist regains control, and by doing this without self-condemnation.

PRACTICE MAKING FRESH STARTS.

Self-Mirroring

To mirror ourselves means to see ourselves accurately. It means to begin where we are, take small steps toward balance and self-care, and notice ourselves taking them. Each step is taken in devotional self-discipline. No step is too small; none is unworthy of our attention.

Think of how a mother responds to her toddler's first unstable steps. She pours on the recognition, and the child soaks it up and goes for more. When we give this kind of attention to our own progress, it motivates and inspires our helplessness, transforming the tendency to collapse into the beginnings of a belief in self-reliance. Even Helpless can manage baby steps!

Helen's entire condo was filled with boxes of papers, magazines, and unopened mail, to the extent that she was ashamed to let anyone see where she lived. For her to accurately mirror herself while she made her condo livable became our strategy for her. The final goal was to have both an uncluttered home and an uncluttered life, but the enormity of this task overwhelmed Helen.

Before we began working together, Helen's only mirroring was from her Perfectionist. She saw only what she had not done and believed she would never do. In her eyes, any first step that she might take was too small to be worthy. The years passed with no changes, as Helen sank further into helplessness and self-loathing. She even stayed with friends and family members because she could no longer bear to be in her own home.

As Helen began to mirror herself more accurately, she focused on the initial goal of emptying one box at a time. This enabled her to sleep at her condo, but she could not yet begin: one whole box was still too much. When she readjusted her focus to the goal of taking the top piece of paper off one box, she was able to begin. From there she worked her way down through the top inch of papers in that box, and eventually through the whole box. She noticed her progress, and felt inspired to do another entire box, then several boxes. Soon, she couldn't wait to get home and work on clearing her entire living room. Thrilled by that success, she invited a friend over, confining him to the room that she had cleared.

When Helen occasionally slipped into creating more clutter, she noticed it without self-condemnation and began again. By recognizing the value of each small step of her progress, she was able to reach one goal after another. She completed in months a task that her Perfectionist had been unable to accomplish for years. Helen successfully fostered herself through this domestic project, and the changes permeated her entire life experience.

TAKE SMALL STEPS, THEN NOTICE THEM.

The Difference Between Collapse and Surrender

The Perfectionist pushes to the point of either collapse or surrender. If it is collapse, the individual succumbs to despair or depression. If it is surrender, the individual accepts the present circumstances and asks Inner Guidance what to do about them. When we are in collapse, we condemn the situation, give up on it, and follow the Backslide. When we surrender, we open ourselves to receive the life force.

Sometimes collapse precedes surrender. That's okay; it's never too late to surrender. Surrender is not weak. It's not failure, even though it sometimes feels as if it is. Surrender is a shift from one state of consciousness to a deeper one.

I used to lose my keys a lot. I'd drive myself crazy frantically searching for them. Each time it happened, I knew that if I would just sit down and meditate for a couple of minutes I would find them. But that always felt like accepting defeat. I had a choice: I could collapse, miss my meeting, and be depressed all day, or I could surrender to the part of myself that knows where my keys are. Finally choosing, I would let go, breathe, make my request, and enter the Void of meditation. Within a couple of minutes, I'd see in my mind's eye the location of my keys.

PRACTICE SURRENDERING ON THE SMALL THINGS,
AND BE INSPIRED TO GO FOR MORE.

10

Calling on the Unconscious

Most of what we know about the brain concerns the cerebral cortex—the rational mind or "thinking cap." The cortex is the brain area that controls the sorting of information that comes in through the senses. We rely on this information to make our decisions. Worries and disturbing thoughts that arise in the cerebral cortex cause stress that affects the entire physiognomy. This "rational" part of the brain is wrapped around nonverbal, prerational portions that date from earlier in humankind's evolution. The cortex sends instructions to these other areas, as well as to the muscles, the organs, the nervous system, and the rest of the body.

The ancient portions of the brain cannot receive verbal instructions from the cerebral cortex, for they develop when movement and sensory perception make up our immediate reality—before we have language to mediate these experiences. These ancient brain parts contain our healing centers and regulate the automatic body functions, such as breathing, heart rate, hormones, and emotions. This is why it is so difficult to control emotions with thoughts, or to stop fear and anxiety simply by telling the mind to stop its thinking. We cannot tell a red, embarrassed face to stop blushing.

The healing centers in the older portions of the brain are beyond the Perfectionist's domain. These centers are reachable only in ways that are beyond the rational; they can be impacted by the use of processes that invite direct sensory experience. Meditation, hypnosis, dreams, and many other states of altered consciousness bypass the cortex and directly enter the healing centers. The use of dance, music, yoga, drumming, gardening—anything that feels like play—is also an excellent way to communicate with these parts of the brain that control change. These modalities are all conduits for Inner Guidance—the communications that we receive back from the healing centers, filtered through the cerebral cortex so that we can understand them.

My clients and I make a point of employing some form of unconscious process in our personal therapeutic work. This chapter highlights some of these processes. You may have others of your own, for there are many more.

Keep Breathing

Ram Dass (one of my favorite teachers) has said that if we could choose only one thing to do for ourselves, it should be to breathe. We know that the autonomic nervous system controls our breathing to keep us alive, but the breath has even further purpose and value.

When we experience depression, anxiety, or fear, the breath becomes so shallow that it seems to stop. One of the best ways to either self-calm or self-enliven is to breathe with the simple intention of being calmed or enlivened. Automatic breathing is mindless. To access the parts of the brain that control healing and change, we need to bring mindfulness and intention to our breathing.

Once I was so terrified before giving a public talk that I couldn't keep my voice from trembling. I spent a few minutes focused on slow, deep belly breathing, and calmed myself almost to the point of sleepiness. There have been other periods, when I have collapsed into depression and Helpless has prevailed, that I haven't wanted to get out of bed in the morning until I've breathed myself into a more alive state.

Then there was the time in a single-engine plane, when my friend the pilot and I came close to crashing. The plane couldn't get enough altitude to clear the mountain range dead ahead, or enough speed to turn around. The hot wind bounced us like a ball in the sky. My friend's voice yelled (an octave too high) for me to stay calm. I didn't want to add my fear to his, so with great determination I breathed away my fear, then calmly watched as we just barely cleared the mountaintop.

Remembering to breathe helped me to cope with these trying situations. There is no trick to this; the breath is a natural resource, and anyone can use it. Why don't more of us use conscious breathing in everyday life? Because there is opposition, within, even to the taking of a breath.

Focused breathing requires us to come into the moment. The Perfectionist dreads that, because it loses control when we become calm. Helpless doesn't want to bother breathing because it's too much work; it wants someone else to breathe for it. The breath is a vital source of life force. Helpless and the Perfectionist are part of the Backslide. Their function is contrary to that of the life force, and their very existence is threatened when we breathe.

Focused breathing, then, is probably the easiest way to weaken the Perfectionist and inspire Helpless into activity. Breathing is frequently overlooked and undervalued because it is so basic, yet it is a natural balancer that tunes us up or down—whichever is needed.

REMIND YOURSELF TO BREATHE,
AS OFTEN AS YOU REMEMBER.

The Value of Meditation

Meditation is not the only way to engage Inner Guidance, but it certainly helps. I use the term meditation loosely, to mean any of various forms of reflection and relaxation that are not drug-induced. Any type of conscious stillness is useful in relieving stress and mental chatter. Even the practice of taking "minute vacations" from anxiety and obsessive thinking can help immeasurably.

Meditation is a little dip into the Void. Its practice is a journey into Essence, often carrying us easily through forces that would otherwise act to keep us out. There is a type of meditation for every personality, and the rewards are great for time spent in stillness. Meditation is a proven method for balancing an active life.

Christine reported to me that, after a few months of Zen meditation practice, she'd had a remarkable experience. While lying on her front lawn one day, she felt a wave of warmth and well-being envelope her. She likened it to being held in a man's arms, because that was her only association on that level of pleasure—and the only way she had thought she could ever feel that happy.

Prior to the experience, Christine had not wanted to challenge her perfectionism because she thought it was the best part of her. However, she sensed that the experience had come through the absence of her habitual uptightness. It made her much more willing to explore her inner world.

Meditation practice fosters intuition, mediates pain, cultivates the fair witness, and promises wisdom. It is a method chosen by many to develop the 92 percent of the brain's capacity that science says remains unused.

Western medicine is beginning to recognize the value of meditation. Some mainstream hospitals now conduct classes in stress reduction and meditation for patients who are not being adequately helped through traditional medical approaches. These meditation classes enable people with chronic disabling pain to return to normal existence—not always free of pain, but in a state of mind in which pain coexists with serenity. Why wait until all else fails before trying meditation?

WHAT FORM OF MEDITATION BEST SUITS YOU?
ARE YOU WILLING TO PRACTICE IT?

Dream Work

Dreams are a potent form of Inner Guidance, for they reveal our predicament and—often—our solution. A dream is most vivid the moment we wake up, and if we don't write it down it usually disappears. Dreams can help us identify the Perfectionist, and they often point the way to freedom.

The following is a dream I had when I asked to be shown my Perfectionist:

A familiar person keeps changing shape. Initially it has the role of protector advisor. I think it helps me and I am very loyal, but it is too intense. It feels cloying. I study it to learn what it is. I watch it change shape until it becomes a kind of vampire. I try to get away from it, but I can't. It shouts an order and I shout back, "No!" Instantly the scene changes. I'm falling headfirst from a tall tower to certain death. I yell as I fall, "Okay!" Instantly the scene changes back again. The creature's face gloats at me. It thinks it has won my fealty by showing its power, but instead I realize that its only power is the power of illusion. I practice withstanding the attacks that come when I refuse to obey its commands. A train speeds toward me and I let it come, trusting that it is an illusion. The train disappears in front of me as I suspected it would. Then the character and the dream fizzle out, just as the Perfectionist does when we discover what it really is.

In this dream, my Inner Guidance was telling me that the Perfectionist is a master of disguises. It makes me think I need it. It controls my experience by using my fear against me. It can make me feel as if I'm dying when I'm not. If I practice treating it like an illusion, it loses power over me.

When we decide to work with dreams, it may serve us better to write down only the ones we want to remember, lest the Perfectionist turn dream work into another burden. Each part of a dream corresponds to a part of the psyche. One way to interpret them is to become curious about the various parts and to let intuition bring their meaning to us. With practice, we will develop our interpretive skills and strengthen our connection to Inner Guidance.

WHAT DID YOU DREAM LAST NIGHT?

Learning to Enter the Void

Before Inner Guidance shows up, an experience of "nothingness" can be expected. No one can predict what it will take for Inner Guidance to get through to the conscious mind or how many obstacles are in its way. While we're waiting, it seems as if nothing is happening. This nothingness is the Void, a sacred stillness somewhat like the gestation period before childbirth.

The Perfectionist hates the Void and tries to avoid it, considering it at best a waste of time, and at worst a horrible emptiness. Addictions and distractions give us ways to forestall the Void, but it can't be shunned forever. In time, when we have had sufficient experience of the Void, we will come to value it.

I wish that our Western society sanctioned the Void, so it wouldn't seem so hard on everybody. It can be thought of as the bridge between the personality and Essence, the core of the creative process, the conception of creation in the inner world prior to manifestation in the outer world. The Void can last anywhere from seconds or minutes for small matters, to weeks or months for larger ones. It is the unknown, that necessary period of not knowing and not doing before one can know what to do.

We suffer unnecessarily, in that space of time when we are switching our allegiance from the Perfectionist to Inner Guidance, because we don't know that "nothing" is what is supposed to happen.

Gail had been fighting cancer for several years. She had become a warrior woman, hell-bent on living a full life. She won her battle: tests showed there was no longer any trace of cancer in her body. At first, she felt exalted, then she hit the Void.

At this point Gail was no longer a woman fighting cancer, but she didn't yet know who she was. The Void was the natural space between who she had been and who she was to become, but it represented a crisis for her until she understood its purpose. She was to live with little self-definition, through a gestation period of unknown length, until she birthed her new self.

The Void teaches patience, compassion, receptivity, and appreciation for simplicity, all of which defuse perfectionism. The passage through the Void can be an uncomfortable one, even when we choose to enter it. And it can be especially challenging when, as in Gail's case, it chooses us.

ENTER THE VOID. PRACTICE NOT KNOWING.

Reparenting and Inner Child Work

Working with our own different aspects and subpersonalities makes use of unconscious processes and accesses the healing centers of the brain. This work is not rational; it is experiential. Through it, we can heal the past and change the future.

Reparenting is something I chose to do for myself, knowing that I would need help in learning how to do it. I didn't know how to care for myself—certainly not as a loving parent would care for a child. I thought the best way to begin would be to find out what kind of care grows a healthy child; perhaps the same care would work for me. I took into consideration the shape I was in from my previous lack of self-care. In other words, I was not starting with a brand new baby, but rather with a wounded child who had a long memory of broken trust. It would take time for my inner child to believe that my motives were benevolent.

Reparenting and inner child work have been well covered in many good books. Some of my clients have attempted to work with these materials and have failed. Although I've known these books to be very effective, I've come to realize that the clients for whom they didn't "work" had yet to connect in a real way to their feelings about themselves.

Some just wanted to "fix" the inner child, to stop it from embarrassing them in public by being too loud or too needy or by causing them to feel socially frozen from extreme shyness. When we feel shamed or angry regarding the child inside of us, our first need is to make genuine contact with our inner child, to show our interest.

Attention and honesty constitute the first step in reparenting, because they develop the trust needed to repair the adult-child relationship. If we follow the "how to" steps in the books before we are willing to give honest attention, our results will be disappointing. If the child doesn't trust the adult's intentions, it cannot find the courage to make contact.

For example, Jocelyn followed the instructions in a book on the inner child to write the following dialogues with her child:

Jocelyn: "I love you, and I want to know what you need."

Inner child: Silence.

Jocelyn: "If you fall down, I will pick you up."

Inner child: Silence.

Jocelyn: "We will talk every day and get to know each other."

Inner child: Silence, followed by a response that Jocelyn felt she made up to get the ball rolling: "OK, Mommy, I want to get to know you too."

Jocelyn quickly lost motivation for inner child work because she couldn't feel a connection. The child inside her could not respond, because Jocelyn didn't mean a thing she said. Jocelyn needed to take time to observe the child through her imagination. And, before the child could begin to trust, it needed some honest attention, not just meaningless platitudes.

Fred was the life of the party. He performed and entertained from a need to be accepted. Although he could brilliantly charm a room full of people, he didn't know when to stop. His excesses would eventually cause him to lose his audience and feel pathetic.

I asked Fred to visualize that unacceptable part of himself that his performances were covering. He imagined himself opening a closet door. Inside was a creature covered in moss and slime. It wasn't human. Sores oozed all over its body, and its eyes couldn't stand the light. The creature couldn't bear to be seen, and Fred was repulsed by the sight of it. It had been shut away for so long that contact was impossible.

Fred's first step with this locked-away creature was to pay attention to it. He needed to do nothing more at this point—just show interest. Gentle curiosity activates Inner Guidance and begins the process of reparenting. Then the next step reveals itself. Fred agreed to let his creature emerge from the closet. In his imagination, he occasionally checked to see how it was doing. His attention caused the moss to dry up and some of the sores to heal. Eventually the creature began to have human skin, and became a boy who looked back at him. Fred's social behavior reflected these changes. He feared that he'd lose his edge, but instead he kept his audience.

Reparenting requires that you begin where you are. If you can't stand the child part of yourself, that is where to begin.

In my own reparenting process, I kept a picture of myself as a young child on a shelf at the foot of my bed. When I felt depressed in the morning, I'd see "her" picture and tell her, "I'll get out of bed for you." I kept other childhood pictures around the house to remind me why I needed to go to the store and eat healthy food. It was for "her." I had looked bright and alive in my early childhood pictures, and I wanted to feel that way again.

PLACE CHILDHOOD PHOTOS OF YOURSELF HERE AND THERE
AROUND THE HOUSE. NOTICE HOW YOU FEEL
WHEN YOU LOOK AT THEM.

Heart Work

The core of heart work is compassion, which is not quite the same as sympathy. As it is most often used, sympathy means having pity, feeling sorry for. Compassion is more about giving respect, concern, regard, and thoughtfulness—all the things we want from other people but often withhold from ourselves.

When compassion directs the inquiries, Inner Guidance brings maximal clarity. Inner Guidance is developed over time, through trial and error. Without compassion, the learning curve is too rigorous to endure. Compassion allows for the awkwardness and uncertainty inherent in the growth of any new skill.

Two models of the compassion principle are Mahatma Gandhi and Francis Bacon. I choose them because they are extreme opposites. Gandhi represents the light and Bacon the dark, yet one can learn from both of them.

Gandhi titled his autobiography *My Experiments With Truth*. He didn't expect himself to know the truth before he practiced something new. He trusted and followed his inner voice even when the stakes were high and he might be making a mistake. Instead of berating himself for not knowing in advance, he would say, "That experiment failed miserably," and move on to another. Gandhi was not afraid to be a fool.

As a young lawyer, Gandhi decided to reduce expenses to save his sponsor's money. He starched his own shirts for court appearances, and cut his own hair. When he appeared in court, his hair was a fright and his shirt puffed starch all over his suit. People laughed at his ridiculous appearance. His response was to agree that it would be more appropriate not to do his own hair and shirts, but he noted that there was value in the entertainment he had provided his peers. Gandhi set a good example in his compassionate allowing and forgiving of his own mistakes.

For those who say that Gandhi had more self-empathy than we because he was so evolved, let's go to the example of Francis Bacon, the self-destructive painter. Bacon relied on the principle of the "controlled accident" to create his best works. It appears that he mostly loathed himself, but he was able to find a compassionate part to direct his creative process.

Bacon's paintings often turned out strangely different from what he originally intended. In creating his art, he surrendered to his Inner Guidance, not knowing what would happen but expecting a surprise. Because he did not inhibit his accidental and often grotesque images, his paintings seem to reflect a process of moving through his own private hell to find a measure of freedom and self-acceptance. His works are brilliant, largely because he accepted them the way they came out and did not censor them. He trusted that whatever wanted to come out of him had some inherent value.

As Francis Bacon demonstrated, heart work doesn't necessarily mean we have to love ourselves. It means that there is a part of us that values and grants permission to whatever wants to come out of us, while we're working out the rest. We are all works in progress; we may as well be fully expressive ones.

WHAT KIND OF SURPRISE WANTS TO JUMP OUT OF YOU?

Spiritual Work

The words Spirit, Truth, Love, Life, and God are different terms for the same concept: whatever it is that evokes a reverent feeling within us. These terms and others like them denote humankind's sacred principles. We can each derive great satisfaction from imbuing our life with the spiritual values represented by these principles, and from engaging in some form of personal spiritual work.

When I say "spiritual work," I'm not referring to a particular thing that we do. I'm referring to the way we live when we embrace a sacred principle and imbue each day's myriad choices and activities with it. Spiritual work begins with the way that we treat ourselves and others in each moment. I have observed that the refusal to include a sacred principle in our daily living causes a severance between our aspirations and our actions. This schism then hinders our ability to make dreams come true.

We see this in the woman who wants a higher degree but can't finish her final paper; the man who needs capital for his business but can't begin his proposal; the actress who wants work yet won't go on auditions; the bachelor who wants marriage and family yet perpetually avoids intimacy. Sometimes major achievements are made under these circumstances, but they bring no fulfillment.

Spiritual work builds a bridge between the big ideas and the small daily actions. It distinguishes the drive of the Perfectionist from the promptings of Inner Guidance, and exposes the differences between the forward-moving life force and the contrary Backslide.

When we are in inner conflict, spiritual work helps us discover which side of the conflict, if either, is life-supported. Perhaps a desired goal is being driven by blind ambition, image perfectionism, or Helpless's rescue fantasies. In such an instance, the Backslide can restore grounding. Or perhaps our goal is life-supported, and the Backslide is a manifestation of Self-Deprecation or Self-Destruction. Sometimes the Backslide is on both sides of a conflict, its intensity obscuring the forward force. When this happens, we can't really discern what we are doing until we see ourselves doing it.

When we notice a disparity between what we're wanting to do and what we're actually doing, that's the time to call on one or all of the above-mentioned sacred principles for support. We can then use the guidance we receive to make needed corrections in our goals or our daily choices.

WHAT IS YOUR SACRED PRINCIPLE?
ASK IT TO DIRECT YOUR DAILY CHOICES.

11

Perfectionism and Your Career

"What do I want to be when I grow up?" This is the question we ask ourselves over and over again, throughout life. This question digs up primal hopes and fears: hope that the answer will be given and our destiny fulfilled before it's too late; fear that it will not be in time, that life will be a disappointment.

We need to build a bridge between fear and hope. To do so calls for identifying both sides of the bridge and then finding a bridge builder. This bridge builder is not to be found anywhere "out there," in the world. It will be found within, and the bridge that we are to build will take us precisely where we need to go to find self-fulfillment.

What we become in the outer world is an extension of our interior world. Who are you in your own mind? Are you someone who believes you can do what you set out to do? Take stock of the parts within you that support you to undertake risk, and the ones that do not. Feel, hear, and sense them. Let them come into your awareness, however it is that they do this.

Believers and Disbelievers

Find the one that knows what you want and says YES! to you. Find the one that is afraid to know, because it is scary to act on our own knowing. Find the one that says, *You can't.* Find the one that says, *What you want is not important enough* or *What you want is too important.*

Who do you think you are? Find the one that says, *It's too late* or *It's too soon—I'm not ready.*

These voices, senses, feelings, are inside of most everyone. The difference between the individuals who reach for what they want and the ones who don't is the response given to these inner voices. Are you going to prevail, or are you going to let your fears take you down?

You know how frightened you are on the inside. It is natural to believe that others are less afraid, but nearly everyone is frightened. Not everyone, however, believes the fear. Don't wait for fear to disappear before you move ahead, for it never will. Separate from your fear, or drag it along with you. One way or another, begin to move.

In activating yourself, you must find the part within that can support you along your way. If you want to break into a world that has been keeping you out, then break into yourself first. Find the believer inside of you that can consummate your chosen destiny. Find this interior advocate and anchor yourself to it. Let it hold you, comfort you, and inspire you to face your interior disbelievers. This is essential if you plan to turn your dreams into reality. Prepare for your own form of holy war.

Getting to the Source of Career Conflicts

In the working world, the Perfectionist can be both a blessing and a curse. It is a principal player in getting us hired, fired, promoted, sidetracked, or applauded. If you want to take a look at how your own career is affected by your Perfectionist, you might begin by considering the following questions.

- Do you feel scapegoated, not trusted, invisible, disrespected, overburdened, underutilized?
- Does someone else claim the credit that belongs to you?
- Are there times when you think sudden death would be too good for your boss?
- Do your employees sometimes seem like a bunch of ingrates?
- Are you beyond bored with your work, but afraid to reach for more? Or afraid to start over? Or afraid to go back to what you really love, and gave up for "practical" reasons?
- Is your Perfectionist a hindrance to your career, or is it an enhancement?

Once you understand that your Perfectionist is at the core of these questions or conflicts, you can answer or resolve each one of them. Once you have identified the nature of your own specific perfectionism, you can begin to make it work for you instead of against you. And once you understand the Perfectionist in other people (see Chapter Seven: When Two Perfectionists Collide), you can defuse the power that they may now seem to wield over you.

Through this discovery process, you will learn exactly what kind of care and feeding your Perfectionist needs to make your career as exciting and fulfilling as you dare to let it be.

Peak Performers

Nearly all of us want to achieve to our highest potential. We can learn something about how to do this from others who have done it. I used to have false assumptions about world-class achievers. I assumed that they were better than me, that they were favored with better circumstances, or that they pushed themselves harder than I pushed myself. I was wrong on all counts. Studies do indicate, however, that the highest achievers are aware of something that I didn't know: they know that they don't have to be perfect.

Charles Garfield, the author of *Peak Performers*, conducted a study of more than two hundred people who had been named by their peers as top performers. Through interviews, questionnaires, and biographies, he learned the shared characteristics of world-class achievers. Included in the study were Albert Einstein, Winston Churchill, Linus Pauling, Luciano Pavarotti, and Mother Teresa.

Dr. Garfield discovered the following common elements in these individuals: They have a passionate commitment to a mission, vision, or sense of purpose. The results they achieve are mission-driven, not goal-driven. They are not obsessed with perfection, nor are they workaholics. They practice self-renewal, relax and reflect on a regular basis, and use their imagination as a mental rehearsal to prepare for action and events.

Peak performers achieve self-mastery through self-knowledge, and rather than being competitive or secretive they tend to be cooperative team players. They have the mental agility and flexibility to make course corrections, and are capable of change when necessary. They can delegate responsibilities and say no to diversions.

Ultimately, the secret to the success of peak performers is that they let themselves be human. As Dr. Garfield says, "Extraordinary achievers are ordinary people who have found ways to make a major impact."

Impressing "the Community Within"

In the working world, one of the most common mistakes we make is to turn our employers, employees, clients, and co-workers into pseudo family members. Through these associates in the workplace, we then act out the emotional conflicts of the past.

Notice how you want your boss, clients, and others to trust you, respect you, approve of you, and treat you fairly. Notice how angry and hurt you become when that doesn't happen. An excellent way to become truly successful in your world is to let go of the need for trust, respect, approval, and even fair treatment.

I'll grant you that it's impossible to release these needs completely, but it is possible to learn to care considerably less what anyone thinks of you. Why? Because what you think they think of you is only your own opinion of yourself, anyway.

You have already wasted enough energy in worrying about and trying to control what "they" think of you and how they treat you. This energy can be put to better use in fueling you to the fulfillment of your dreams. I suggest that you give up these fruitless pursuits, and turn instead to what "the community within" thinks of you. That's where the only control is to be found.

The No-Agreement Exercise

If we can impress "the community within," we can master our entire world. Years ago, a certain exercise in a seminar I took drove home this truth for me. Each person had to take a turn standing in front of the group of forty participants and telling a story or revealing something intimate. The group was instructed to heckle, ignore, ridicule, and otherwise do everything possible to try to get the speaker to collapse. Each speaker was instructed to do anything necessary to find agreement on the inside, in spite of a total lack of agreement on the outside.

Can you imagine how frightening and powerful this exercise was? It was painful to watch the ones who quit on themselves, and exhilarating to see the ones who held up and kept going. There were also some who pretended to hold up, but really only wrapped themselves in a facade of confidence. I saw the difference between the ones who were held back by internal rules and the ones who made new rules for themselves as they went along.

When each person ended his or her story, the group was asked to comment on what they had seen. The ones who supported themselves and held up were cheered and applauded in true celebration, for that's what we all want to be able to do. The ones who collapsed, or only pretended to hold up, were given the opportunity to process their emotional experiences.

In the workplace, as in every other aspect of life, the gravest crimes are not the ones committed against us but those we commit against ourselves. Once we have acknowledged these perpetrations, we need more self-support than ever, to forgive ourselves for the times of self-abandonment so that we can return to balance. Once balance has been restored, we can begin again to manifest our dreams of an ideal career. We can do this by resuming our all-important search for "the community within"—the ones who wish us well, the ones who will move mountains in our behalf.

Dig Deep to Reach High

That benevolent, supportive "community" exists in each of us, and is accessible as Inner Guidance. We can find this guidance, expand it, and follow it to great benefit. Once this wisdom is summoned, it sustains us through all the worldly battles. Once enough respect, trust, approval, and fairness is found on the inside, it miraculously appears on the outside.

You might as well stop waiting for your boss to give you the approval your parents never gave you. Struggle instead to find this approval within yourself, so that you can weather the no-agreement exercise. If you can elicit this self-approbation, you'll subsequently be surprised to see how often you get the treatment you've always wanted. For the secret of receiving "strokes" of any kind is that we must first give them to ourselves.

Once you have your self-support system firmly in place, you can begin to reach for all that you want. The reach will require personal power—enough power to withstand the ones who will envy you, compete with you, and make you the object of their hostility. When your associates do these things, you will no longer react to them as if they were your family members failing to approve of you. You will see these individuals more accurately: as people whose behavior reflects—not you—but themselves, and their own battles from their past.

To put these ideas in other words, if you want to reach high in the world, then first dig deep. Next, find out where you want to go, and compare that to where you currently are.

If you want to change careers, you may need to make peace with the idea of taking an entry-level position in your new career, then working your way up. The time that is often wasted in resisting starting over from scratch is more than enough time to start over, move up, and be well on your way. All in all, starting over is much less painful than the stall against starting over. Rather than stagnating in an unhappy position and feeling your life force seep away, allow yourself to move forward toward something that you want.

Allies in Your Holy War

Declare what you want to be, do, and have, then find your internal support and guidance. Identify your opposition: your own forms of perfectionism and helplessness. You will also find these opponents in the working world, waiting to challenge and irritate you. But these adversaries serve a good purpose. They are the people in your day-to-day life who can show you the state of your relationship with yourself. Find the allies out there with whom you can exchange support. They are reflections of the well-wisher within.

Armed with your holy war resources, begin to set the course of your future career. Keep some of your attention on balance, slowing down or speeding up when necessary. Distinguish when you need to struggle and when you need to not struggle. Stay open and flexible for course corrections. Check your self-importance, making sure you laugh at yourself enough along your way. Leave a generous margin for trial and error. Let yourself fall down, then get up, lick your wounds, and begin again. Remember to break the rules that have previously limited you, so that you can live the rest of your professional life as full-out, wide-open, and fearlessly as you dare.

12

True Stories
From My Clients

M y clients are courageous people. They are willing to see their secrets revealed in the pages of this book, if it will support others in the struggle toward self-acceptance.

The following are some of my clients' stories. The names have been changed, along with any elements that could allow these individuals to be recognized, but the stories are true. They are descriptions of the real work that we have done together.

Each case illustrates three or more types of perfectionism, listed in order of severity. That is, the first type mentioned has the most influence over the individual and the third type has the least. I found, in working with these clients, that initially my specific references to perfectionism did not go over well. (As we know, the Perfectionist dreads exposure.) Later these individuals came up with their own names for their perfectionism. Some of the designations given were "The Scourge," "Ms. Gritch," "The Petty Tyrant," and "Mother Superior."

Early in the therapeutic process, we discovered the characteristics of each subpersonality and the body feelings that accompanied it. Following that, the self-awakening process was unique to each person, as each was drawn to different methods of accessing the unconscious (e.g., dreams, inner child work, or hypnotherapy).

The stories cover all the types of perfectionism that I have listed in Chapter Four, as well as the following consequences: debt; depression;

isolation; alcoholism; eating disorders; job burnout; self-mutilation; the inability to engage in relationships; and addictions to sex, money, cigarettes, and relationships.

Jillian: Stubbornness, Self-Deprecation, and Righteousness

Jillian, forty-five, lived in her intellect and had a history of aloneness. Her self-expression was devoid of emotion, and she showed disdain for job associates, family members, and past therapists. Although attractive, she seemed worn down by her many years in the film industry. She worked long hours under pressure, and had little time for sleep, friends, or regular meals. Life was about surviving each job, recovering from it, and finding another one.

Jillian's world view was one of disenchantment. Her air of superiority distanced people. She made enemies without realizing it, for she didn't see the negative impact her behavior had on others. Eventually, she stopped rising in her profession. When I first met her, Jillian was unemployed, and incapacitated by poverty, panic attacks, and Chronic Fatigue Syndrome. Under her exhaustion was an obvious deep resentment for the way her life had gone.

Jillian's mother, a volatile prescription drug addict, had neglected her children. Her father, an emotionally vacant physician, had focused his attention on keeping his wife happy, at the expense of the children. Jillian's fervent efforts to be good enough to receive her parents' love and care were futile. Either she was the object of her mother's anger or she went unnoticed by both parents.

Gradually Jillian quit noticing her mother's dissatisfaction, which set her pattern of tuning out. She turned her attention away from people and feelings to fixate on tasks, becoming a stickler for details. Jillian got her self-esteem by not being emotional or needy like her mother, but this adaptation eclipsed the development of her natural self.

Jillian's forms of perfectionism are Stubbornness, Self-Deprecation, and Righteousness. The stubbornness developed in protest of her intolerable home life. The self-deprecation stemmed from a certainty that, no matter how hard she tried, she would never be good enough, which gave rise to a depression that took over her life. Instead of addressing her depression, she worked even harder. When her personality caused her to be fired, she would miss the point, thinking, *I couldn't have worked any harder. I didn't even take lunch breaks.* Finally,

Righteousness gave Jillian a purpose: being right. Her fixation on details obscured the big picture, causing poor priority setting. She became increasingly intolerant of fellow workers and resentful of authorities. She wanted to be right and to stand her ground.

Jillian eventually collapsed into the helplessness of illness. Fortunately, the breakdown made her more willing to search for the source of her failures. But before she could launch a self-inquiry, Jillian needed more balance. She needed to be energized by external support until she could access her internal support system.

Throughout our work together, Jillian also received holistic health care. She was strengthened by the diverse support she received, especially because it all pointed her in the same direction: toward balance and faith in her own spirit.

She learned to reassess her choices and priorities. So many of her choices were driven by Self-Deprecation's fear of not being good enough that she became skeptical of them all. Righteousness was a false source of self-esteem that had allowed Jillian to feel right by making others wrong. Stubbornness was a strong Backslide; its fear of change kept her from seeing clearly.

Among Jillian's discoveries was a realization that her urgency to speed up was actually a signal to slow down. She was sobered but undaunted to observe how she brought about her failures. Commitment, practice, and humor helped her to make keen self-observations. I keep a basket of animal slippers at the entrance to the office, to help clients relax and set the mood for their work. Jillian's favorite choice was hot pink flamingos; she felt silly and little-girlish in them, and they helped her laugh at herself.

Jillian watched herself act out her belief in the futility of her own efforts. She tracked the difference in her behaviors when she acted for and against the belief, which gave her a new sense of having power to affect her circumstances. She explored her early injuries, sorting the past from the present so her current responses would fit her current experiences.

Because Self-Deprecation had long ago forced her into an output-only mode, Jillian had to learn how to receive. In our sessions, she was able to open her receiving mechanism by breathing and becoming curious about the subtle occurrences within her. She called these exercises "rummaging" her way to a contact with Essence.

Through rummaging, Jillian discovered needs and feelings. She began to follow the sense of wonder and aliveness she felt inside her body. The first time she wept in my office, Jillian touched her tears and said with delight, "Oh look, I'm crying!"

Her inquiries revealed the questions she needed to ask to soften the Perfectionist and access Inner Guidance: "Do I want to argue with my boss and be right or get along with him and be successful? Am I giving precedence to the goal at the expense of others when I ignore my colleagues' concerns? Is it a drain on my energy when I read the entire newspaper?" An important self-discovery loosened the hold of her Stubbornness. She told me, "If I don't do enough of what I want, I won't want to do the responsible things."

Jillian gradually changed her relationship to higher-ups by becoming her own authority. She learned to let her employers know the consequences of unrealistic requests, saying in a neutral manner, "Would you like me to stop doing what you gave me this morning in order to do what you're giving me now? That may result in a missed deadline. Here is a choice of solutions."

As of this writing, Jillian is able to feel her feelings instead of having panic attacks. Her chronic fatigue is well in remission. As her relationship to herself has changed, so have her personal and professional relationships. She loves her job, and revels in self-care by giving herself lovely vacations and hiring someone to run errands and shop for her groceries. She enjoys doing less and being more. Her expression has gone from deadpan to radiant. All is not perfect, of course, but Jillian now has the inner resources to master her challenges.

Kathy: Arrogance, Martyrdom, and Greed-Envy

Kathy, thirty-one, was a recovering alcoholic who had achieved several years of sobriety through Alcoholics Anonymous. She was very open and personable, with a quick smile and keen sense of humor. Kathy had ready access to a childlike sense of trust, wonder, and magic. She was also like a raw nerve ending: exquisitely sensitive, and subject to emotional extremes such as severe depression that caused her to miss several days of work at a time. She was newly divorced by choice, yet still admittedly addicted to her ex-husband.

Fear that she would never be loved kept driving Kathy back to her former spouse. Each time, she rediscovered how damaging such reunions were for both of them. She would force herself to leave again, then fall more deeply into depression, condemning herself for her weakness.

Kathy's father is a practicing alcoholic, and the family revolved around his moods. Imperfection became anything that upset Dad or the family peace. She told me, "In my family, if someone has an imperfection, you fix it—or ream them for it." Kathy was frequently reamed for not being perfect. She felt that she lost her family's love whenever she showed her real self.

Kathy's mother was easily overwhelmed, and intolerant of conflict. She said that Kathy was the only reason she didn't kill herself, so Kathy felt certain that if she ever expressed negative feelings she would kill her mother. She was the little performer in the family, and could always be counted on to make everyone feel better with her cheerleader kind of enthusiasm. Kathy felt a growing rift between her family role and the real self that she had to hide, even from herself. She wanted everyone to be happy, but felt increasingly depressed and frightened behind her smile. Both parents relied on Kathy to create peace in the family, so she learned to ream herself when she failed to do this.

When Kathy found her Inner Guidance through AA, her family felt threatened, for her changes upset the old status quo. She was caught in the Perfectionist's double bind: if she behaved autonomously, her family attacked her for having a mind of her own and she lost their love. Then Kathy attacked herself. If she sacrificed her truth to keep their love, she betrayed herself, then attacked herself for that. Kathy repeated this family dynamic in her marriage and her job. She felt nonstop pressure to be the star performer. Depression, a brief respite from torment, was often her only way out.

Kathy's forms of perfectionism are Arrogance, Martyrdom, and Greed-Envy, fixated on love. Arrogance covered her real self and buffered her family's attacks. Though AA helped her make great strides in her ability to receive support and show her emotions, Arrogance continued to punish her for the imperfections that disrupted her family. Martyrdom demanded that she sacrifice her self-care needs to keep the peace, in exchange for love from her parents, and Greed-Envy caused her addiction to love.

Because peace had to prevail at all costs, Kathy had never fostered the self-love that could sustain her during conflict. Any choice she made that disrupted the peace was a betrayal of her family. Each time her parents withheld their love, she felt as if she would die. She could sense even minor ripples in their feelings toward her.

Kathy's strongest resources were her sense of humor, the support she received through AA, and her higher power. These elements had subdued Arrogance by the time I met her. Through twelve-step work, Kathy had developed a deep faith that served her well. Her higher power was her sacred principle, and her sense of wonder was quite resilient. She was willing to be vulnerable—something Arrogance doesn't permit. But she needed a lot of mirroring and support to confront the vicious Perfectionist within her.

Kathy readily acknowledged her perfectionism, which she sometimes called "Dad." By listening to her self-talk, she learned how to support herself. Instead of just feeling abused, she began to enjoy catching her Perfectionist in the act of attacking her.

Kathy discovered a secret belief that said, "Feelings can kill." She used hypnotherapy to let her Inner Guidance take her on healing journeys, and learned that feelings might make you *feel* that you're going to die, but they can't kill you. This strengthened her capacity to uphold herself through painful emotions.

She gained a lot of self-knowledge regarding her susceptibility to the Perfectionist. Her most severe self-attacks concerned her addiction to her ex-husband. She consistently redirected her attention from need for his love to self-acceptance. Once she stopped forcing herself to let go, she was surprised at how naturally she could detach, and this further strengthened her confidence. Before a family visit, she identified the ways her family caused her to lose her sense of self, and planned how to counter their predictable moves. Humor kept this fun for her, as she reviewed her choices of mildly daring to super-daring responses.

Kathy realized that she was missing work because she had to be perfect there, too. Arrogance needs to appear "together." If she felt depressed, it would show, and her boss wouldn't love her anymore—so she stayed home. The missed days drove her boss crazy, but because Kathy was an exemplary employee she didn't fire her. With the help of her sense of humor, Kathy used daring behavior to dramatically improve her attendance. "Dare to be half-assed" became her new motto. She changed her goal from "Be perfect at work" to "Just sit in the chair," and her job performance was not diminished.

Watching changes in the way she related to people she sponsored in AA, Kathy noticed her Martyrdom dissolving. She developed more faith in each person's Inner Guidance, and stopped feeling the need to fix or take care of them. She no longer struggled to set limits; she just set them. She was greatly relieved to realize that sponsoring others didn't wear her out anymore.

One of the most caring things Kathy did for herself was to accept her Perfectionist. She knew she would never be fully rid of it, but she could learn how to live with it. That shift in attitude marked the end of her serious troubles with perfectionism, because—just like every other part of us—the Perfectionist needs acceptance, too.

A new relationship confirmed how far Kathy had come. The relationship became a place to win even more of her autonomy. After all of her self-work, Kathy decided to become a therapist. She returned to school, where she was a star student and intern. She had conquered so much internal pressure that her new learning curve was a pleasant process. Kathy swiftly excelled in her new career, for she no longer had to drag the weight of the Perfectionist up the ladder with her.

Florence: Martyrdom, Self-Deprecation, and Stubbornness

Florence, a fifty-year-old divorcee, came into my office severely depressed. Her every move, even taking a breath, seemed an enormous effort. She was overweight, and very angry with herself about it. Florence had lived her life as a bohemian. Her hair was in big auburn curls, she wore bold, lively prints, and she was known for her wild earrings. Her laugh was hearty and infectious. Florence had a way of putting everyone at ease, but she never saw this about herself, or felt at ease herself. To others, she seemed a free spirit, but she was filled with guilt and self-loathing.

Florence had done many wild and crazy things in her life, with little enjoyment. She had an inner authority that forbade her to fully enjoy herself, an internal law that said she should accomplish more in the world, do more for others, and not think of herself. Florence's pattern of overgiving to others and rarely having energy left for herself was her way of abiding by this law.

Florence's mother was a talented woman who had never developed herself. Her insecurity had caused her to divert her worldly ambition into raising her daughter, whom she blamed for the sacrifice. She still exerted powerful control over Florence. Florence's father had frequent, incapacitating depressive episodes. He avoided his wife and showered love on Florence, which widened the existing rift in the family.

Florence bore the brunt of her mother's jealousy, resentment, and criticism. Her mother viewed Florence as her chance to compensate for her own failed life, but her need to live through her daughter was at odds with Florence's essence. Further, her mother thought love meant worrying, helping, and making improvements, whether Florence wanted this or not.

Florence needed to be seen as good enough already—not her mother's work in progress, in continual need of repair. Since nothing she could be or do was good enough for her mother, she chose a rebellious, unconventional lifestyle. To make up for the love she wasn't receiving from her mother, she turned to food and cigarettes. Food also served as part of her rebellion, since her mother abhorred overweight.

Florence's forms of perfectionism are Martyrdom (to feel worthy and win her mother's love, she became like her mother), Self-Deprecation (she believed her mother's mirroring that she was not good enough), and Stubbornness (her rebellious power struggle was a fight against her mother's control).

In our work together, Florence discovered her self-defeating pattern. Like her father, she is subject to depression. When her depression lifts, she seems transformed. She falls in love with life and nature, but can't sustain it. Her Perfectionist puts her on a harsh self-improvement regime: she quits smoking, starts a strict diet, and plans to organize her life. Self-Deprecation then insists that she's not good enough to succeed. It makes unrealistic demands and withholds support.

Martyrdom will not let Florence give less to others and more to herself. This prevents balance, and she becomes angry that she can't follow through. The attempt to fix herself is a reenactment of her mother's treatment, which still serves only to activate her Stubbornness. Her rebellion against herself triggers her guilt and drives her into depression once again. Her Stubbornness refuses to see this pattern, out of fear that she might have to change it.

Florence's dream life was so vivid she enjoyed seeking the nightly messages. Her dreams revealed her internal struggle, pointed her toward freedom, and gave her the mirroring she needed to strengthen her trust in her essence. To restore her original nature, Florence needed to sort the free part of her spirit from the rebellious part. The latter was a response to her mother's tyranny, and now it blocked her from living fully. Her overly ambitious side was the Perfectionist, a representation of her mother's tyranny in action within her.

Florence felt that she had wasted her life. The reason she had let so much time go by was that she perpetually felt she must change herself before starting to live. She kept saying, "When I'm thin, when I'm organized, when I stop smoking, then I'll live my life." Nothing I or anyone else said could penetrate this belief system. Fortunately, some clear messages to the contrary came to her through her dreams.

The dreams helped her identify her forms of perfectionism, and encouraged her to wake up to her false ambition. They taught her how to see herself more clearly, pointing out to her the small steps she was already taking. The dreams gave her the mirroring she had sorely missed throughout her life.

Florence opened to Inner Guidance and her sacred principles. She began to questioned her desire to change herself so that she could live her life, and decided to give to herself instead. She quit the job she hated, took a different job, and found a new home surrounded by nature. She learned to actually enjoy setting limits and saying no to the requests of others, and thus gained more energy for self-care. As she started believing that people really cared about her, she began receiving support from friends and allies.

Slowly, Florence's eating, self-care, and organizational habits improved. We had referred to her weight problem as the final frontier, and finally she was there. Instead of starting another strict diet, she became more aware of her eating habits in the moment, and her extra weight began to come off naturally. Florence noticed that upsets did not send her to food for comfort as before. Rather than trying to change herself, she had changed her relationship with herself, and that had changed her relationship with food.

Another positive outcome was a transformed relationship with her mother. Instead of obeying and placating her mother, Florence began to speak her mind. Instead of criticizing, her mother backed off and lightened up. Florence was astounded when her mother said, "You're the best daughter a mother could have." Once she stopped needing her mother's approval, Mom gave it.

Now that she had less to prove to others and more to give to herself, Florence started her own lucrative business, one that allowed her to work at home. Another change that occurred was less expected: she fell back in love with a man she had loved in the past. He was less ambitious than she, which she had not been able to accept before, but he loved her for herself. This time, Florence was able to disregard her Perfectionist and accept his love.

Michael: Greed-Envy, Self-Destruction, and Righteousness

Michael was a startlingly handsome man of thirty whose self-expression was controlled and unrevealing—more like a representation that was designed to give a desired impression. Michael clearly described his goals: he wanted to go through a reparenting process to heal his childhood, and also wanted to determine if his lack of sexual interest in women was because he was gay or because of his bitter resentment toward his mother. He said that, during sex with men, he was often unable to sustain an erection, preferring voyeuristic and exhibition-istic masturbation. It took tremendous courage for him to disclose this information.

Michael's mother, an alcoholic, had selected him from among his siblings to provide her with the closeness she and her husband didn't share. Michael's father, a minimal participant in the boy's life, allowed his wife to dominate the household. The mother fused herself to her son, telling him what to think and feel, and showing intolerance for any differences between them. Unable to say when she was happy or hurt, she chose instead to keep Michael informed as to when he was right or wrong. Her method of giving and then withdrawing love taught him exactly how to behave. Each time she took away her love, he felt loneliness and shame.

Michael's forms of perfectionism are Greed-Envy fixated on attention and approval, Self-Destruction, and Righteousness. Greed-Envy emerged from the pattern of his mother being too close and then withdrawing her love when she disapproved of him. Michael became so addicted to approval, while always braced for the loss of closeness, that he lived in hypervigilant awareness of others' responses to him. His resentment was aroused whenever someone else received praise or he didn't get enough attention. He learned to monitor his own behavior even more closely, and certainly more harshly, than his mother had.

The inability to sustain an erection during sex was a consequence of Michael's perfectionism. When someone desired him, his need for approval caused him to experience that desire as a demand: *I have to keep you liking me, so I must do what you want.* This "demand" impaired his freedom, which caused him to lose his desire. Because he didn't feel safe enough to say no, he was unable to feel his "yes."

In going along with the wishes of others, he was only obeying his need to be liked, and he could find no pleasure in that. If he let go in the sexual experience, he might lose control and be engulfed as he was by his mother. This conflict drove him to masturbate in risky settings as a controllable substitute for intimacy, a choice that took him further into addiction and away from his essence.

Michael adopted his mother's Righteousness. By determining that others rarely met his standards, he kept himself from emotionally connecting. Since he presented himself according to a prepared script, he was disturbed when circumstances required him to be flexible. Righteousness feared he might make a mistake—a crime punishable by self-rejection. Michael's Perfectionist kept him in isolation and then attacked him for feeling lonely. It gave him very little margin to be human, and he knew this. Fortunately, he had a strong desire to reparent himself and be free, and a great willingness to do whatever that would take.

Discrimination was the early focus in Michael's work, as he needed to identify his actual feelings and needs. He also needed to develop boundaries to separate his sense of himself from other people, especially his mother. He gave himself guidelines to follow (no bringing someone home on the first meeting) because he could not yet distinguish his own wants from another's. He realized that his inability to sustain an erection during sex was only his body telling him he was not emotionally ready for intimacy.

Michael became his own doting parent, watching his growth process with fascination. His guiding principle was his core self, for he wanted more than anything to be real. He identified his Perfectionist and keenly tuned in to his body, receiving Inner Guidance through physical sensations. When he asked himself questions, the tightness, pressure, or dissonance in his body—or any change in those sensations—gave him his answers.

Zen meditation was a powerful tool for Michael. While meditating, he practiced returning his attention to his breath whenever he noticed a thought. This was a metaphor for listening to the Perfectionist's commentary and then returning to the Self.

Michael needed self-acceptance regarding his sexual preferences. He decided to grant himself permission to be gay, whether or not he was. After some exploration, he enthusiastically "came out" to family and friends. Even though some of his sexual activities were self-destructive, he stopped trying to change them and started trying to learn more about them.

His review of the factors preceding each sexual event revealed the driving force behind his addiction: profound loneliness combined with self-judgment. He realized that change could not occur until the safety and pleasure of intimate sex bested the thrill of anonymous encounters. His deepening self-connection increasingly braced him through his attacks of loneliness. He could process his own feelings, instead of acting them out sexually. That awareness allowed him to reduce his sexual focus and attend to the business of living more fully.

Michael was a natural student. His love of learning gradually overcame his fear of not knowing and making a mistake. He enrolled in a holistic health course that gave him the challenge and structure he needed to further heal his childhood wounds while he developed his sense of purpose. His Perfectionist plagued him by demanding that his school papers be written with more expertise. He countered his perfectionism with daring behavior: "Dare to write a C paper. Dare to turn the paper in late. Dare to not know what you're talking about."

His school's group activities helped him to further work out his need to be the center of attention as he went beyond his self-interest to experience an interest in others. His self-presentation became more spontaneous. He began having intimate and pleasurable sexual experiences. Simultaneously, his destructive sexual activities diminished.

A major transformation brought about by Michael's work was in his sense of humor—especially his ability to laugh at himself, which lightened the heaviness of his Perfectionist. His new sense of humor was also reflected in his ability to laugh at his mother's idiosyncrasies instead of feeling wounded by them.

Michael became a devoted holistic health practitioner. Giving service lifted him out of his self-consciousness and connected him to others, deeply fulfilling him. He came to see that there had never been anything wrong with him except his fear that something was wrong with him.

Patricia: Self-Destruction, Self-Deprecation, Stubbornness, and Image Vanity

Patricia, thirty-nine, was a poised and graceful artist who came into my office with downcast eyes, as if she were already taking too much of my time. She said was incapable of having a relationship, because men terrified her. She had been depressed for as long as she could remember. Before long, she told me a secret she had been carrying for years: that she couldn't stop trying to destroy herself.

Patricia spoke of a strict religious upbringing, of being forced by her father to kneel and pray for the souls in purgatory until her knees bled. She was told that the blood was atonement for her sins. Later in life, she would whip her own back and cut her chest in an attempt to bleed herself pure again. Patricia had been anorexic as an adolescent, a condition that went unnoticed by her elders and went away when she started the beatings. She considered her body to be deformed.

Patricia's mother had been continually depressed and withdrawn, and had left when Patricia was ten. Patricia's father, an alcoholic, had ignored her until his drinking sent him into "religious" experiences. Patricia had essentially raised herself, but saw no harm in that. She thought that she not only should have raised herself, but should have lifted her mother's depression and made her want to stay in the home. She also believed that, if she had been a good child, she wouldn't have needed punishment.

Patricia has four types of perfectionism: Self-Destruction, Self-Deprecation, Stubbornness, and Image Vanity. Patricia's Perfectionist was an annihilator who found everything about her bad. Her every move was wrong, so Self-Destruction would tear her down in an attempt to rebuild her in its own image. Self-Deprecation continually gathered evidence that, no matter how extreme her efforts, she was not good enough. Stubbornness was unwilling to view her as innocent of any wrongdoing; everything was her fault. It feared any change in her perspective, especially one that might shed a less-than-favorable light on her parents. Patricia's Image Vanity had lost much of its power by the time I met her, but her perceptual distortion had caused her to make extreme attempts to perfect her body through exercise and unnecessary cosmetic surgery.

Upon telling me her secret, Patricia felt immediate relief. Her Self-Destruction had weighed heavily on her for many years, keeping her isolated, and now she needed to speak of her shame and self-loathing. She beat herself because she hated herself, and hated herself because she beat herself. She could not yet accept me as an advocate for her innocence; if I spoke for her goodness, she would speak for her badness. Her Stubbornness initially refused a psychiatric evaluation, but she eventually went, and was given medication that subdued the frequency and severity of her self-beatings and slightly lifted her depression.

Patricia's perfectionism was near the extreme end of the intensity continuum. I needed to approach with caution, to work around her Stubbornness, for meeting it head-on only fixed it more firmly. Self-Deprecation needed to be approached gently too, or it would trigger Self-Destruction's need to punish her for having a positive thought about herself.

I found it imperative never to push Patricia to remember anything, lest she become overwhelmed. She did have faith in the Holy Spirit, and that faith would activate her Inner Guidance. Her vivid dream life and amazing artwork proved to be the doors to her essence. Her dreams began to clarify her Perfectionist, which she named The Scourge. She learned through dreams that The Scourge was an annihilating force that expressed itself through her self-beatings and self-hatred. Her dream figures included a journalist who kept an unbiased record of her dream events; this was the emergence of a fair witness.

Self-care was difficult for Patricia because she felt unworthy of it. Her self-attacks often came when she was overly tired, hungry, or anxious. She felt her body signals but ignored them; a kind of amnesia convinced her that her self-attacks were behind her and balance was no longer necessary. She began putting notes around the house to remind herself to eat, sleep, and breathe, even if she thought she didn't need it.

Zen meditation gave Patricia more objectivity. It worked for her because it is an impersonal discipline and she didn't have to like herself to do it. In the beginning, it seemed less like self-care than a penance that she was willing to pay. Guided-imagery tapes left her cold because they were too loving.

Patricia needed to replace her self-attacks with something healing. When she felt them coming on, she began to channel them into her art by painting ghastly and violent images. Sometimes the attacks passed; at other times she only delayed them. Patricia brought her paintings to my office so that we could talk about them to discover their messages. Her work began to show such images as healing wounds, gashed body parts with stitches in them, or one sliver of light shining on an exhumed grave.

Patricia had no friends or allies—no support system. She needed some people in her life who could reduce her feeling of being a misfit, and also needed to explore the basis of her behavior. She accomplished both aims by going to twelve-step meetings for Adult Children of Alcoholics. At this point, a benevolent Fairy Godmother appeared in her dreams to coach her through frightening dream events. In one dream, she proclaimed her innocence to The Scourge. This marked a shift in her ability to access her inner well-wisher.

Over time, Patricia was able to consider the possibility that her parents hadn't given her what children need to foster self-esteem. Slowly she accepted the idea that she was treating herself as she had been treated. She saw that the absence of a caring mother and presence of an abusive father had kept her from developing an internal self-nurturer.

Patricia's inner life and outer circumstances have dramatically improved. She has formed friendships and become increasingly able to speak up for herself. As of this writing, she has had two art shows that led to a well-paying job as an art director. She is not yet ready to let a man into her life, but she recognizes that she is increasingly able to receive good fortune. She still has occasional self-attacks, but is able to comfort herself afterward instead of staying trapped in self-hate. Patricia is learning to live with her perfectionism, which has reduced its power over her and freed her to feel some peace in her life where formerly there was only torment.

Jennifer and Doug: Arrogance, Stubbornness, and Greed-Envy Married to Self-Deprecation, Impatience, and Greed-Envy

Jennifer and Doug were both in mid-life crisis. They had been married for thirteen years, and were at a crossroads in their marriage and their individual careers. Tension was tearing at their closeness. Their commitment to each other was strong, but something had to change and they both knew it.

Jennifer was a social worker with an artist's heart who seemed not to know how creative and beautiful she was. Her original goal had been to help save children, but after fifteen discouraging years she resented the children in her caseload and was angry at herself for failing. She continually tried to prove herself by volunteering for extra work and then felt angry and ashamed when she couldn't do it. Exhaustion from overwork left her little energy for herself or her husband.

Doug was a master of understated eloquence. He had the magnetism conferred by an exceptional intelligence that is humbly expressed. Doug had burned out of three professions, deciding each time that the type of occupation was wrong for him. He didn't see that his way of approaching any work would burn him out. Doug worked long, hard, and fast. He worried about wasting time and not getting enough done, and resented Jennifer for excluding him from her emotional life.

As a couple, Doug and Jennifer walked softly around each other to protect each other's feelings and prevent conflict. Each felt so much responsibility for the other's happiness that they couldn't relax enough to feel the depth of their connection. Both had a skewed relationship to money, and they colluded in their overspending. Doug's rationale was, "I'm providing for my wife," while Jennifer's was, "My husband didn't tell me not to." Neither accepted accountability for their own spending, and they had mounting debts. Doug invested time and energy in money-making endeavors that contributed more to his burnout than to his income.

Jennifer had been raised in a poor family. She felt like a have-not, and longed to be among the elite. Her mother had been subject to breakdowns and erratic emotional outbursts that diminished her ability to nurture. Jennifer had lived without a space of her own. She had felt continually exposed and deprived of the privacy she needed, for she had a fertile creativity that required sanctuary and time alone.

Jennifer's types of Perfectionism are Arrogance, Stubbornness, and Greed-Envy fixated on physical and emotional security. She had felt extremely vulnerable as a child, because she never knew when her mother might come unhinged. Arrogance had emerged as a protection against her vulnerability and her fear that she might be ordinary, or crazy like her mother. Jennifer was so determined to improve her lot in life that Stubbornness engaged to focus her efforts. Greed-Envy for emotional and physical security arose to reduce the suffering she could not directly acknowledge. She filled her deprivation with such substitutes as food, purchases, and looking good.

Doug learned at an early age that he was mentally gifted, and his religious upbringing caused him to feel a responsibility to use his gifts to help others. His intelligence allowed him to excel in school effortlessly, but he could not appreciate his successes because he believed he had fooled everyone into thinking he was good. How could he be good if he wasn't even trying? Two events launched Doug into premature adulthood: his mother died after a long illness, and then his father lost all of his money in a series of failed investments. Doug's sense of responsibility made him feel guilty for wanting to be a kid. He became a do-gooder to suppress his forbidden self-interest and feelings of loss, but instead of going away these mutated into a craving for money.

Doug's types of perfectionism are Self-Deprecation, Impatience, and Greed-Envy fixated on financial security. Self-Deprecation arose when Doug felt as if he were continually failing to live up to expectations. Impatience tried to help him by urging him to do more in less time, so that he might eke out a little something for himself. Greed-Envy for financial security emerged from his deprivation and childhood loss. Combined with Self-Deprecation and Impatience, Greed-Envy caused him to attempt financial shortcuts that resulted in even higher debt.

Jennifer's and Doug's types of perfectionism intermesh with each other, although they at first had difficulty sorting it all out. Doug felt shut out from Jennifer's real feelings. His Self-Deprecation feared it was because he wasn't good enough, when actually Jennifer's Arrogance, fearing exposure, was telling her that if she let him in she might be seen as ordinary or crazy

Both Doug's Self-Deprecation and Jennifer's Arrogance cared about appearances. Doug's concern was, *Do people think I'm good enough?* Jennifer's was, *Do people know I'm extraordinary and not crazy?* Each reinforced the other's need to look good, which further drained their energy and prevented them from fully accepting themselves.

Jennifer's Stubbornness collided with Doug's Impatience. In conflict, Impatience wants to hurry and get over it and Stubbornness wants to avoid the conflict entirely. This causes Impatience to grow more frustrated, so that it makes Stubbornness even more obstinate.

Greed-Envy pulled on both of them. Each felt responsible for the other's happiness, but Greed-Envy is a deep hole that no one else can fill. Its fear of loss choked their emotional honesty, and interfered with their efforts to feel the intimacy they both wanted.

Jennifer and Doug were out of balance, lacking faith in themselves and their marriage. They tried too hard to keep everything together, out of fear that it would fall apart. Fortunately, they were eager to discover their self-deceptions and to develop Inner Guidance. They were strongly aligned in their intention to learn what they were really doing. God was their sacred principle. Both were caught in a conflict between the Perfectionist (God from their childhood) and their essence (the present connection to God). Mid-life crisis was a wake-up call for each of them. Their goal became: "Let this marriage be my vehicle to awaken."

Jennifer

We learned early on that, in her work with me, Jennifer tried to be good. She wanted to report good things to win my approval. She named her Perfectionist "Ms. Gritch"—a dictatorial, witch-like character—then began to study Ms. Gritch's patterns.

Whenever she tried to be good or to avoid the bad things, Jennifer's leg would start swinging, and the truth-seeker within her caught on to this. I worked with Jennifer and Doug on the telephone, as they lived out of state, so I would not have known about her swinging leg if she hadn't told me.

Jennifer's willingness to speak the truth was a powerful resource for her, because it defused Arrogance's fear of exposure. She often started a session with, "What do I not want to talk about?" By naming her resistance she defused Stubbornness.

One of the things she didn't want to talk about was her shopping sprees. Greed-Envy's feeling of lack caused her to buy things on impulse. She looked at these events honestly, and restored balance by returning the unneeded items, even if it embarrassed her to do so. She found out how much money she and Doug owed and took a more active role in reducing the debt. These were acts of courage, because they challenged her fear of lack, her fear of change, and her need to look good.

Jennifer's attempts to be all things to all people left her exhausted and resentful. She participated in Doug's get-rich-quick endeavors, even when she didn't believe in them, because they both feared that if they didn't do everything together, something had to be wrong with their marriage. Every time Jennifer refused Doug, she felt like a bad wife and a selfish person. But she couldn't go on pleasing, because she needed to be true to herself. So she carved out some time for rest. She went through several rounds of finding balance, followed by taking on too much again, followed by exhaustion. After each Gritch attack, she would begin again, and each round brought her more self-knowledge about her natural rhythm.

Jennifer gave herself some time alone to cultivate Inner Guidance. She created a set of personal oracle cards, and used them to receive mirroring and messages. She also created a meditation practice for herself, a guided visualization. Her journeys to a sacred place put her in touch with the different parts of herself and their influences.

She was ready for daring behavior. She pulled back at work and risked losing her star status, which challenged Arrogance because it brought her too close to the ordinary. She pulled out of her husband's financial endeavor, an enormous challenge to Greed-Envy's need for emotional and physical security. Her withdrawal challenged Doug's need to look good, because public presentation was essential in his work. How could people continue to believe in him if his wife no longer stood beside him? Her growing strength and devotion to herself enabled her to feel the fear and do it anyway.

Around this time I made a mistake in my work with Jennifer: a thoughtless comment about the enmeshment in their relationship, which impaired her connection with me for a while. She started reporting answers to questions she had already solved instead of allowing me into her internal questioning process. I asked if I had done anything to make her lose trust in me.

She spoke of the comment I had made and said how much it had hurt her. I admitted my mistake and said I wished I could promise never to do it again, but I do step in it from time to time. We got back on track, both knowing we neither need nor require each other to be perfect.

Doug

Doug channeled his love of sleuthing and solving puzzles into an enthusiastic quest for self-knowledge. After burning out of three professions, he was quite skeptical of himself. He wanted Inner

Guidance that he could trust. He had innate body wisdom, and he needed that to balance his overly developed intellect. He knew that his facile mind had outsmarted him for years. But his ability to read his own body signals engaged Inner Guidance and began to expose his perfectionism.

Doug called his Perfectionist "That System." He learned its characteristics by using mindfulness in all his activities. After he quit his last job (the above-mentioned financial endeavor), he returned to his original profession, watching for his burnout tendencies. They showed up right away, and he discovered what drove them. Time and again he caught Self-Deprecation and Impatience in the act, and so was able to learn about their roots. Through the body connection, he tracked his Perfectionist's moves without totally falling for them.

Doug enrolled in a new money venture (Jennifer was quick to declare that she would not participate this time), as he wanted to clear up his relationship to money and to work. He brought mindfulness to his actions, which included keeping a record of all his expenditures. He watched That System very closely while he participated in the get-rich-quick program.

He learned that That System fears dying of starvation (Greed-Envy fixated on financial security). Its belief that it will never have enough money causes him to work angles and take short cuts to get it. In truth, these short cuts do not bring money, they take it away. When he does make money, he can't keep it because he feels undeserving of it (Self-Deprecation) because others are less fortunate than he. He quickly looks for ways to get rid of it, often through impulse purchases for his wife.

Once he discovered what he was really doing, Impatience wanted him to get out of the money project right away. But Doug knew that if he got out too fast, he would just do it again. He also saw the value in refusing Impatience's demands. He let himself weather frustration while he waited for Inner Guidance. Doug made a policy to sit with and not act on any decision for at least twenty-four hours. He laughed as he told me, "Boy, that really frustrated Impatience."

Doug studied his financial mentors and noticed that they had the image he valued, but upon closer examination, he saw that they lacked the substance he valued even more. Doug became disillusioned, and got out of the money venture because he had learned his lesson.

His next lesson was at work, where he had broken his money and burnout patterns. His debt was paid off and he earned more money working fewer hours, which confronted Self-Deprecation. But he got no points for not burning out, because he now committed another sin. He earned money he didn't deserve by not working hard enough. He said, "I'm beginning to get it. That System has crazy wiring and will never be satisfied. I might as well please myself."

Gardening was Doug's form of meditation. He spent up to two hours gardening before work each day. Though life now felt too easy for him, he weathered his guilt.

The Marriage

The work each of them had done naturally brought Jennifer and Doug to the challenge of their marriage. They couldn't be autonomous individuals without having an autonomous marriage. They had a pattern of avoiding conflict that was fueled by Greed-Envy's fear of losing each other. Jennifer would avoid what can't be avoided (Stubbornness) and Doug would accept what can't be accepted (Self-Deprecation) until Impatience caused him to erupt.

Now they took more risks to be natural and honest with each other, where they had previously walked softly. They had a period of bumping into each other, while they both worked less to take care of each other. This change brought on a "Should we be together?" discussion. They revealed their doubts, aired their differences, and felt the intimacy of honesty and the strength of their commitment.

Jennifer and Doug recommitted to their marriage. They successfully defused the Romantic Perfectionist, and were relieved to learn that their marriage had always been stronger than they knew. Their increased faith in themselves as individuals allowed them to find this out.

The decision to buy a house challenged both of them, but they were ready. The house search triggered the childhood injury that had originally created Jennifer's Greed-Envy. She had kept at bay her desperate need for a home for so long, that now the need fully blossomed.

Doug had to contend with his urge to buy a house impulsively, even if they couldn't afford it, to please his wife and spare her another loss. But the faith they had built in themselves and each other allowed them to stay in the discomfort until they found the house that was right for them. By having the faith to take their time, they found a beautiful home that they could afford.

Doug and Jennifer both weathered their continual urge to quit their jobs. Both had legitimate reasons, yet they sat tight, through the push of their perfectionism, and waited for guidance.

Through Jennifer's self-care practices, she learned that her heart's desire was to be an artist. She dared to declare this, and it happened. She developed a ground-breaking project in her community that allowed her to be the artist she was. Instead of trying to save the children, Jennifer had decided to save herself.

Her new project, she discovered, enabled her to inspire children. Now when she looks into the wonder of their faces, she knows she reaches them in a way that she couldn't before. Jennifer senses that more change is coming. Now she doesn't only fear it; she also wants it.

As of this writing, Doug doesn't know what will come next. He wants to feel a deeper sense of purpose and service than the one Self-Deprecation generates, and he won't let Impatience move him before he is guided. One day, he stated his intentions spontaneously by saying, "I'm declaring myself open to new perspectives, opportunities, and guidance. I relinquish my pictures. I accept my guidance however it comes, even if it shocks me." That's a lot of faith.

A Promise

I want to make you big promises—assurances of a transformation equal to my own "before" and "after" experience of living inside my skin. (Not that I'll ever get to "after," since the journey never ends.)

I want to say that, if you use the principles in this book, your life will become magical and all your dreams will come true. You will become the person you always wanted to be.

Yet none of this is a given.

It is truer to say that, if you use the principles in this book, your appreciation of life will flourish. That is, if you can let life be different than you thought it would be. Life will probably be far brighter than it appeared in your dark, frightened moments. Yet it will most likely fall well below your highest expectations. This will be a disappointment to the Perfectionist, but an affirmation of your humanness—which is, in itself, good cause for celebration.

Sometimes I laugh out loud at myself, for all my silly ideas of the past and for the foolish notions yet to come. And then I cry from relief, as I gratefully release more of my need to control life and to be special in the eyes of others.

Years ago, I heard a woman describe herself as "just another bozo on the bus." At the time, I said to myself, "What a self-disparaging statement." But it has since become my mantra, when the Perfectionist threatens to get out of hand.

There's one claim I can now make that I could never make before, and it comes as a direct result of Inner Guidance and Essence work.

I love life.

I would like to hear what happens for you.

An Inner Guidance Course

This is a charted course to guide you through uncharted territory. Find a friend or therapist to accompany you, or put together a group to take this course with you. The company of fellow journeyers will strengthen and encourage you along your way.

Before the first meeting, set up your altar (see the Inner Guidance Exercises, page 160) and do the Mirror Exercise (see page 161 of the Inner Guidance Exercises). These preparatory procedures are to be done alone, not with fellow journeyers. Keep a journal to record your Inner Guidance experiences.

Group Guidelines

1. Meetings are held weekly, and require a one-hour minimum for two participants. For a group, allow up to two and one-half hours.
2. Group members agree to keep all personal sharing confidential.
3. Understanding that drugs and alcohol diminish clarity and distort guidance, members agree to refrain from the use of these before and after group meetings and home exercises.
4. Following the suggested time allotments for exercises and group sharing focuses self-expression and reduces the susceptibility to backlash. Give more time to someone whose feelings are up, and stay within limits for stories and other sharing.
5. Begin each group with a brief opening meditation, in silence or with meditation music. End each group with a brief ritual of your choice that connects the group (e.g., holding hands in a circle).

6. When others are speaking, listen to them instead of letting your Perfectionist mentally rehearse what you will say.

7. Before giving feedback to another person, ask if it is wanted. Group members need to feel safe enough to reveal themselves. Save feedback for open discussions.

8. Do this curriculum humanly, not perfectly. If there are some exercises that you just don't want to do, don't force yourself. If members drop out before the end, take some time to process the impact. The loss may strengthen or weaken the group.

The Fourteen-Week Course

Week One

In Your Group or With Your Partner: Have each individual compose an intention statement, declaring the intention to develop Inner Guidance. Write your statement in your journal, in your own words, from your heart. Speak the words out loud, feeling yourself and listening to yourself speak them. The Perfectionist will try to infiltrate your process. It may start by choosing a higher level of commitment than you really feel. Don't try to suppress it, just notice it.

Feel your level of openness and receptivity. Notice the different feelings that come up. They will begin to reveal your Perfectionist. Listen to your partner or to the others in the group as they speak their declarations of intention. Notice whether "the words and music match." Is there a disparity or forced feeling? Are you comparing yourself to others?

Follow with an open discussion of what you noticed about yourself. Share only what you want to share, and only when it feels meaningful to you. Your self-connection is more important than a wish to fit in, look good, or do it right.

At Home: Review portions of the book and do an Inner Guidance Writing Session (see the Inner Guidance Exercises, page 163). Ask yourself the following questions.

What is my relationship to:
- Ambition
- Idealism
- Rebelliousness
- Responsibility
- Guilt
- Struggle
- Suffering

Apply each answer to your real-life circumstances.

Week Two

In Your Group or With Your Partner: Share some meaningful parts of the guidance you received at home (5 to 10 minutes per person). Have a discussion concerning this week's topics, and let it include the giving and receiving of support.

At Home: Begin practicing mindfulness this week. Notice your attitude, self-talk, and body signals. Begin to distinguish the self-talk and sensations that accompany the Perfectionist from the self-talk and sensations that accompany Inner Guidance. Think about what form of meditation practice you would like to choose.

Week Three

In Your Group or With Your Partner: Share what you observed and learned about yourself (5 to 10 minutes per person). Notice if you tried to correct yourself. Change at this point is premature, usually driven by the Perfectionist, and will result in backlash. Use the remaining time for open discussion and support.

At Home: Do an Inner Guidance writing session. Ask yourself the following questions.

What is my level of balance with regard to:
- Work
- Play
- Rest
- Study

Apply each answer to your real-life circumstances.

Week Four

In Your Group or With Your Partner: Share some meaningful parts of the guidance you received at home (5 to 10 minutes per person). Choose a form of meditation practice to deepen your Inner Guidance experience, and share your choice. Practice this meditation three to six times each week for a minimum of ten minutes, working up to a length of time that suits you.

Tell the group or your partner what kind of support you need. Each week, report your level of intention. Remember to be where you are, rather than where you think you should be. If your intention is slipping, say so, and ask for help in finding out what you need. Do you need to change your meditation practice, reduce your length of time? Is the Backslide interfering with your practice?

At Home: Review "Peak Performers" (Chapter Eleven, page 125). Apply the elements of success to your own life experience in an Inner Guidance writing session.

Week Five

In Your Group or With Your Partner: Share what you learned in your writing session, including self-appreciation and changes you would like to make (5 to 10 minutes per person). Use the remaining time for open discussion and support.

At Home: Review, in writing, the following list of fears. Notice the ones you can feel. Notice the ones you don't want to feel.

- Fear of being weak, vulnerable, defective, crazy, etc.
- Fear of being not good enough
- Fear of being perceived as not good enough
- Fear of change
- Fear of unworthiness
- Fear of missing something
- Fear of being wrong, or making a mistake
- Fear of lack, scarcity, or loss
- Fear of losing control

Week Six

In Your Group or With Your Partner: Share some meaningful parts of what you learned (5 to 10 minutes per person). Use the remaining time for open discussion and support.

At Home: Review Chapter Four: Nine Kinds of Perfectionism. Don't try to decide which types are yours. Just notice your different feelings about them. Remember that the Perfectionist doesn't want to be exposed, and can hide itself very well.

Week Seven

In Your Group or With Your Partner: Share some meaningful parts of what you learned (5 to 10 minutes per person). Which kinds of perfectionism do you most not want to have? Use the remaining time for open discussion and support.

At Home: Review Chapter Twelve: True Stories From My Clients. Write your story, and include how you would like your future to be different from your past. Take as much time as you like to write it, then refine it to a four-page maximum.

Week Eight

In Your Group or With Your Partner: Share your story by telling it, not reading it (10 to 15 minutes per person). Allow extra time for feelings, but not stories. No group discussion at this meeting.

At Home: Reflect on each person's story and your feelings about it. Prepare to give feedback to group members or to your partner.

Week Nine

In Your Group or With Your Partner: Tell the people in your group, one at a time, how their stories helped you to understand them. Tell them the ways you feel comfortable and safe with them and the ways you still need to feel more comfortable and safe (10 to 20 minutes per person if in a group, divided into 2 to 3 minutes of feedback for each other individual).

At Home: Do an Inner Guidance Writing Session about the feelings triggered in you during the meeting. Ask to receive self-knowledge.

Week Ten

In Your Group or With Your Partner: Begin again. Declare your intention to develop Inner Guidance. Write this intention in your journal and speak the words aloud. Feel what is true for you now. Has your commitment grown less or more strong? Do you have a better understanding of your process? Perhaps your commitment is cyclical, or naturally wavers with your moods. Notice what factors influence your level of commitment. Listen to the others or to your partner. Compare your present level of commitment to your first commitment, but not to anyone else's. Use the remaining time for an open discussion about what was noticed. Give and receive support.

At Home: Renew your meditation practice by letting each session be like your first. Release expectations or judgments about what you experience while meditating. Choose the length of time that you want to sit. Staying put during that time—no matter what happens or doesn't happen—is the only part of meditation practice that is yours to control.

Week Eleven

In Your Group or With Your Partner: Begin with a longer group meditation. Do a Group Mirroring process in partners (see the Inner Guidance Exercises, page 163). No group discussion at this meeting.

At Home: Do an Inner Guidance Writing Session about the questions or emotions that were triggered during the previous exercise. Notice yourself as you feel and process your responses to the exercise.

Week Twelve

In Your Group or With Your Partner: Give and receive Feedback in response to last week's Group Mirroring process (see the Inner Guidance Exercises, page 164). Use the remaining time for open discussion and support.

At Home: Identify the characteristics of your Perfectionist and give it a name.

Week Thirteen

In Your Group or With Your Partner: Share the name you have given your Perfectionist, and tell what led you to choose this name. Use the remaining time for an open discussion of what each person has learned about his or her type of perfectionism.

At Home: Reflect on your form of Helplessness. Is it depressed, frightened, burned-out, ashamed, paralyzed, lost in fantasy? Does it want to run away? Is it waiting for rescue? How do you feel about it? Do an

Inner Guidance Writing Session (page 163). Ask: "What is my form of Helplessness? What is my first small step? What kind of support do I need?"

Week Fourteen

In Your Group or With Your Partner: Share what you learned about Helpless. What is your first step? What are your obstacles? What kind of support do you need from members of the group? (Allow 5 to 10 minutes per person.)

Now that you have completed the course, the group can either dissolve or continue as an Inner Guidance Support Group. Remember: the steps you take must be small enough for Helpless to manage them. If they are too big, Helpless will collapse, or the Perfectionist will take over to push your process. End this meeting with acknowledgments of self-appreciation and appreciation for fellow group members.

At Home: Do the Mirror Exercise: "The State of the Union" (page 161). This is not an exercise to be shared, but one for you alone. Notice the difference between this and your first experience of this exercise.

Inner Guidance Exercises

Create an Altar to Essence

Giving our attention to the principles we hold sacred fosters our experience of them. Whether your guiding principle is God, Love, Life, or Nature, if you build an altar in reverence, you will be inviting Essence to abide in your life. You can dedicate a quiet corner of any room for this purpose. Fill it with symbols of your sacred principle: pictures, candles, flowers, and beautiful objects from nature.

My altar is a low table covered with a cloth. I sit on a meditation cushion with a back support as I behold my altar and feel my gratitude for Life. Time spent here, each morning or at any other chosen time, calls your sacred principle into your heart and mind to infuse your daily actions. This is time well spent. If the Perfectionist inserts itself into this exercise, it helps to place a symbol for it, as well. It will be better behaved if it, too, is honored and included.

The Mirror Exercise: "The State of the Union"

This exercise instantly flushes out my Perfectionist and reveals the current state of my relationship to myself. I go through this process periodically, to see how I'm really doing.

While standing in front of a mirror, look at yourself and say, "I accept myself unconditionally. Right now."

When spoken aloud while looking at yourself in the mirror, these words reveal the Perfectionist—the part of you that sees your flaws and finds you unacceptable because of them.

Your growing self-acceptance will be mirrored in this exercise, if you do it over time. When you accept yourself, you don't go blind to your flaws, you just don't use your awareness of them to put yourself down. You may want to change things about yourself and your appearance, but these factors are not used as conditions to win self-acceptance. Rather, they are gifts to yourself.

An Inner Guidance Asking Session

I tend to ask for Inner Guidance throughout the day. But if I don't periodically use this exercise, I can be listening to the "guidance" of my Perfectionist without knowing it. This Asking Session is especially helpful when I face an important challenge or need to bring a more focused intention to my questions.

It's important to choose a safe and quiet setting where you will not be distracted. I sit up straight, perhaps supported by pillows, with pen and journal on my lap. Sometimes it adds clarity to first identify what you do not want your answer to be. That answer may be the one you get, all the same. To receive Inner Guidance, you have to be willing for the answer to be one you don't necessarily like.

Remember that the process of receiving guidance is separate from that of following guidance. Once you have received it, often you will need more time to trust it and prepare yourself to follow it. I used to assume that guidance was only true if it was harsh medicine. Sometimes I still have difficulty receiving guidance that I do like; I think I'm tricking myself into hearing what I want to hear. It will take time to identify your specific forms of resistance to guidance, which are directly connected to your types of perfectionism.

Begin by setting your intention to receive Inner Guidance. As you breathe slowly and deeply, imagine yourself opening a bit more with each breath. Feel your willingness to connect to your deeper wisdom. The period that forms the question and the still period that follows is more important than receiving the answer. We have no control over how or when the answer will come, or what the answer will be. We do have control over our willingness and intention to learn.

Begin the process of writing down the question. For example: "I need some perspective on my present challenge/relationship/illness. Please correct any misconceptions I am holding. If I am seeing clearly, please support me to trust myself. I am willing to see my blind spots."

Next, empty your mind to prevent the Perfectionist from expediently answering your question. There is no hurry for answers. The thinking mind only forms the question and catches the answer. It has no role in forming the answer.

Imagine that your mind is a water vessel. See yourself pull the plug at your navel, and watch the water level drop with each exhalation. This will move you out of your head and toward your essence. As you empty your mind, you'll find that you let go of your question, all thoughts about your question, and even past guidance about your question. This creates a "beginner's mind," and an empty space for new guidance to fill.

Sit silently for the period you have set aside (a minimum of five minutes). If you start to have an experience or receive an answer, hold it for a minute before you write it down, so you don't bounce back up to your mind and lose the contact.

If nothing comes during this period, be patient. Go on about your day, periodically reminding yourself of your question. This affirms your intention, and moves you closer to the guidance. Before sleep, if the guidance has not yet come, ask for a dream. Keep your journal and pen near your bed.

In the morning, if a dream came, record it. Then ask your Inner Guidance to explain how the dream relates to your question. Follow the above-detailed process once again, incorporating your dream into the mix. If you do not remember a dream, check to see if you have a new perspective on your question. You may have worked it out during the night.

We need to keep a humble mind about the Inner Guidance process. I like to remember a Buddhist saying: "If you do not understand something, stand under it." It may take time to build a bridge between our conscious and our unconscious mind for the guidance to travel across. We don't know what inner workings have to happen to get it up and running. What we do know is that, if we will just wait, our patience will be rewarded.

An Inner Guidance Writing Session

This is the same as an Inner Guidance Asking Session, with additional time to write your response. Do not censor, edit, or judge your writing. It doesn't matter yet if the response is connected to Inner Guidance. Think of this exercise, initially, as "cleaning out the carburetor." The more you practice it, the clearer your responses will become. When I do a writing session, my responses often begin as platitudes or drivel. It's important to weather the awkwardness or discomfort that accompanies any new endeavor, until a deeper connection is made.

Group Mirroring

Choose a partner and find a spot away from others. Each partner is going to mirror the other's Essence, Perfectionist, and Helpless part. It's important to follow the instructions closely and to refrain from adding any discussion.

The partners sit face to face. One speaks, and the other listens and repeats what was said. This exercise calls for courage and the willingness to hear both compliments and constructive criticism. Prepare to feel emotional reactions, and hold yourself steady through the exercise in spite of them. Your first reactions are not necessarily your true response. To minimize the Perfectionist's involvement, tell your truth and come from a compassionate place, whether giving or receiving.

Begin with three deep belly breaths.

The giver: Say, "This is how I see your Essence," and go on to say what you see.

The receiver: Just listen, and when the giver has finished, repeat what you heard.

The giver: Affirm or correct what the receiver heard.

Take three more deep belly breaths.

The giver: Say, "This is how I see your Perfectionist," and go on to say what you see.

The receiver: Repeat what you heard, without explaining or disagreeing.

The giver: Affirm or correct what the receiver heard.

Take three more deep belly breaths.

The giver: Say, "This is how I see your Helpless part," and go on to say what you see (e.g., depression, immobilization, a looking for rescue).

The receiver: Repeat what you heard. If you disagree, do so silently.

The giver: Affirm or correct what the receiver heard.

Take three more deep belly breaths.

Change sides and repeat the process (unless you are working with a therapist).

The Following Session: Feedback

Last week's receiver to last week's giver: Say, "This is the part of what you said about my Essence that I agree is true, and this is what I disagree with," and go on to say how you agree and disagree.

Then say, "This is the part of what you said about my Perfectionist that I agree is true, and this is what I disagree with," and go on to say how you agree and disagree.

Then say, "This is the part of what you said about my Helpless part that I agree is true, and this is what I disagree with," and go on to say how you agree and disagree.

Through all this, the partner only listens.

If you (the receiver) have gained more self-knowledge about your Essence, Perfectionist, and/or Helpless part, speak about it.

Take three deep belly breaths. Then change sides and repeat the process.

These group exercises can create profound results in your life. The structured safety of the group enables you to look inward and then to express your feelings and reveal yourself openly without fear of social repercussions.

May these exercises, together with what you have taken from this book, contribute to your self-empowerment and your renewed relationship with yourself.

Glossary

ALTAR. A table, often low, upon which are placed personally selected objects that foster a feeling of reverence. Usually the table is covered with a cloth, and such things as candles, flowers, icons, and photographs—whatever opens the heart and centers the mind—are placed upon it. The altar may be a place for meditation or simply a visual representation of an individual's sacred principles.

AMBITION. A desire to achieve a particular end. Ambition needs to be tempered with trust in and respect for the process of achieving that end, so that the fear of failure doesn't overly influence the endeavor. If the process leading to the achievement has balance and integrity, the accomplishment can be savored.

ARROGANCE. One of the nine types of perfectionism. Arrogance is a facade of invulnerability that covers the fear of being vulnerable. It arises to compensate for a feeling of being weak or defective within the self, or alien in one's group. Arrogance is a protection, the need for which was generated by an event or series of events causing an intolerable sense of vulnerability.

AUTONOMY. The level of self-governing that can be sustained by the individual, especially in the presence of authority figures. Compliance and rebelliousness both indicate a low level of autonomy. Sovereignty of the thoughts, choices, and behavior indicates a high level of autonomy.

BACKLASH, THE. A manifestation of extreme Helpless behavior; a collapse or breakdown that follows extreme perfectionism. The Backlash produces a reaction commensurate in strength to the action that provoked it (a too-strict weight-loss diet results in overeating and weight gain, out of a reaction to the severe deprivation).

BACKSLIDE, THE. A natural phase of the growth process that nonetheless frightens the Perfectionist into driving harder or faster to reach its aims. Depending on the underlying fear of the given type of perfectionism, the feeling is of losing whatever is greatly needed (time, gains, strength, control). The Backslide cannot be prevented, but it can be diminished and managed by an acceptance of its inevitability, and by working within its effects. Attempts to resist the Backslide increase its power and hinder growth.

DARK SIDE, THE. The hidden part of the self, the part of the identity that is unknown, disowned, or disliked. Also known as the shadow, it influences choices and behavior without the individual's awareness, until it becomes known.

DISGUISE. A falsely assumed appearance or identity. The Perfectionist has many ways to deceive the individual into thinking it is one thing when it is really quite another. These are its disguises.

ESSENCE. The pure nature of anything. In this sense, the personal core of the self. Essence is an archetype, universal to all people, and is also known as the soul or higher self. It is the purest part of each person, the part that is well, wise, free of the wounds of personality, and deeply connected to life, love, God, and truth.

GREED-ENVY. One of the nine types of perfectionism, induced by the fear of loss, lack, or scarcity of something specifically needed, and generated by an event or series of events in which loss was actually experienced. The fear of loss usually has a specific fixation related to the nature of the original injury, and is not general in nature. Examples: the fear of not having enough love, knowledge, money, success, approval, or beauty.

GUILT. The feeling of having committed an offense or breach of conduct. The Perfectionist uses guilt as one of its disguises, falsely causing the individual to feel as if he or she has committed (or is about to commit) an offense. The guilt is often associated with an act of self-care, especially one that requires saying no to the needs of another.

HEART WORK. Endeavors undertaken with a loving, heartfelt attitude. Compassion, self-acceptance, an open heart, and a healthy respect for the challenges faced are essential in the making of changes or learning of something new.

HELPLESS. An archetype of powerlessness that exists within the psyche of all humans; the feeling of having no internal support or personal power, and of being unable to meet whatever challenge is faced. The Helpless aspect manifests in different ways for each person (depression, collapse, defenselessness), in degrees of intensity ranging from mild episodes of helplessness to a severe inability to function. At its extreme, the Helpless archetype corresponds to the American Psychiatric Association's diagnosis of the Borderline Personality Disorder.

IDEALISM. A virtue often distorted by the Perfectionist. A standard of excellence that, when used as inspiration, supports one to see and reach for transcendent possibilities. The Perfectionist misuses idealism to impose a minimum standard of acceptable achievement. Anything less is deemed a failure.

IMAGE VANITY. One of the nine types of perfectionism, arising from the fear of being perceived as not good enough. Image Vanity strives to make a good impression on "those who matter," with efforts to achieve the right "look" or reputation at the expense of substance.

IMPATIENCE. One of the nine types of perfectionism, arising from the fear of missing something. It causes a striving to rush into the future, and results in a missing of the present. Impatience derives from the recollection of past disappointments, and from the feeling that there is not enough time to experience or achieve whatever is desired.

INNER GUIDANCE. An internal source of compassionate wisdom that empowers and supports the individual with clarity and direction. Inner Guidance may come in thoughts, inspiration, or intuition; it may be heard, seen, or sensed. It is the abiding truth-teller, yet it is sometimes confused with the Perfectionist, which gives invalid, disempowering advice.

MARTYRDOM. One of the nine types of perfectionism, arising from the fear of unworthiness and causing one to overcompensate with acts of "helping" in an effort to prove worthiness. Martyrdom generates from an overemphasis on what one does for others, at the expense of focusing on who one intrinsically is. There is great difficulty in receiving from others, unless what is being received is recognition for what one has already given.

MIRRORING. Having one's identity reflected, as if one were looking in a mirror, by another person. Begins at birth with the parents, and soon forms the individual's identity. If original mirroring was inaccurate, this creates a mirroring injury and distorts one's self-perception.

OBSESSION. Invasive, compelling thoughts—often mistaken as Inner Guidance—that cause a feeling of urgency. Usually accompanied by uncontrollable compulsive behavior.

PERFECTIONISM. A disposition to regard anything short of perfection as unacceptable. This personality trait usually manifests under conditions specific to the individual, whenever self-doubt causes overcompensation.

PERFECTIONIST, THE. The part of each individual's personal psyche that regards anything short of perfection as unacceptable. Each person's internal Perfectionist, rooted deeply in the psyche, seeks perfection in ways stemming from the particular personal injury that created a marked self-doubt.

PSYCHONEUROIMMUNOLOGY. A maturing science that studies the relationship of the personality to health. It postulates that thoughts and emotions directly affect the nervous system. The responses of the nervous system affect the immune system, which determines overall health. These connections can be utilized to improve health and to retard or reverse the progression of illness.

REBEL, THE. An archetype for the part of the collective psyche that is needed to win autonomy from authority figures. One needs to be able to say no to important others to find one's truth. The Rebel becomes a problem within the psyche when the individual confuses it with freedom. True freedom comes from the ability to first say no to authority figures and then say yes to oneself.

REPARENTING. A self-designed course in returning to childhood for the purpose of raising oneself all over again with a more optimal style of parenting. Becoming one's own wise, benevolent, supportive parent.

RIGHTEOUSNESS. One of the nine forms of perfectionism, arising from the fear of being wrong. It causes a stern judgmentalism toward the self and others when a perceived mistake has been committed. Righteousness generates from the individual having lived in a fault-finding environment.

SELF-DECEPTION. A state in which one withholds the truth from oneself through a form of trickery. Self-deception is rarely intentional; the individual tends to unconsciously adjust the facts until they fit what he or she is predisposed to believe.

SELF-DEPRECATION. One of the nine types of perfectionism, arising from the fear of not being good enough. It causes one to overcompensate and try harder to prove oneself, especially to important others, who are deemed better people in the eyes of Self-Deprecation. It originates from a childhood atmosphere of criticism and of lack of appreciation for the child's strengths and accomplishments.

SELF-DESTRUCTION. One of the nine types of perfectionism, arising from the fear of losing control. It causes behaviors that bring an immediate feeling of increased control, and it ultimately leads to a breakdown of some kind. Addictions flourish within those individuals whose form of perfectionism is self-destruction.

SELF-ESTEEM. The feeling of good will or level of self-acceptance that one has for oneself, ranging from high to low depending on the early mirroring. Self-esteem can be raised by accurate present mirroring.

SELF-IMAGE. The picture or view that one holds of oneself. It may be fairly accurate, if the individual had adequate mirroring as a child, or highly distorted if there was a mirroring injury.

STUBBORNNESS. One of the nine types of perfectionism, arising from the fear of change. It causes the individual to refuse to consider other points of view, and to overcompensate by clinging to the status quo. Stubbornness is generated from a belief that change, if it is allowed, invites disaster.

TRICKSTER, THE. An archetype of the part of the collective psyche that causes one to strongly perceive the truth as one thing when it is actually something quite different. An internal deceiver that forces the individual to learn the truth by making mistakes of an often embarrassing nature.

Bibliography

Adams, J., editor. *Reclaiming the Inner Child.* New York: Jeremy Tarcher, Inc., 1990.

Bowen, M. *Family Therapy in Clinical Practice.* New York: Jason Aronson, 1978.

Cameron, J. *The Artist's Way.* New York: Putnam Publishing Company, 1992.

Castaneda, C. *The Fire Within.* New York: Simon & Shuster, 1991.

————. *The Art Of Dreaming.* New York: HarperCollins Publishers, Inc., 1993.

Chopich, E. and Paul, M. *Healing Your Aloneness.* New York: Harper-Collins Publishers, Inc., 1990.

Chopra, D. *Quantum Healing.* New York: Bantam Books, 1989.

Dallet, J. *Saturday's Child.* Toronto: Inner City Books, 1991.

Elliot, M. and Meltsner, S. *The Perfectionist Predicament.* New York: William Morrow and Company, 1991.

Erikson, E. H. *Identity and the Life Cycle.* London: W. W. Norton & Company, Inc. 1980.

Erickson, M. and Rossi, E. *Hypnotherapy.* New York: Irvington Publishers, Inc., 1979.

Estés, C. *Women Who Run With the Wolves.* New York: Ballantine Books, 1992.

Gandhi, M. K. *The Story of My Experiments With Truth.* Washington, D.C.: Public Affairs Press, 1948.

Garfield, C. *Peak Performers.* New York: Avon Books, 1986.

Gendlin, E. *Focusing.* New York: Bantam Books, 1981.

Hardin, P. P. *What Are You Doing With the Rest of Your Life?* San Rafael, CA: New World Library, 1992.

Jampolski, G. and Cirincione, D. *Change Your Mind, Change Your Life.* New York: Bantam Books, 1994.

Jung, C. G. *Psychology and Religion.* New York: Yale University Press, 1938.

———. *Memories, Dreams, And Reflections.* New York: Random House, 1974.

———. *The Undiscovered Self.* New York: Little Brown, 1974.

Kabat-Zinn, J. *Wherever You Go There You Are.* New York: Hyperion, 1994.

Keyes, M. *Emotions and the Enneagram.* Muir Beach, CA.: Molydatur Publications, 1988.

———. *The Enneagram Relationship Workbook.* Muir Beach, CA: Molydatur Publications, 1991.

Klein, M. *Envy and Gratitude.* New York: Basic Books, 1957.

Kohut, H. *The Analysis of Self.* New York: International University Press, 1971.

Kopp, S. *Back to One.* Palo Alto, CA: Science and Behavior Books, 1977.

Leadbeater, C. W. *The Chakras.* Wheaton, Illinois: The Theosophical Publishing House, 1927.

Maslow, A. *Toward a Psychology of Being.* New York: Von Nostrans Reinhold Company, 1971.

———. *The Further Reaches of Human Nature.* New York: Penguin Books, 1972.

Masters, A. *The Way of The Lover.* Canada: Xanthyros Foundation, 1988.

Masterson, J. F. *Psychotherapy of the Borderline Adult.* New York: Brunner/Mazel, 1976.

———. *Narcissistic and Borderline Disorder.* New York: Brunner/ Mazel, 1981.

———. *Countertransference and Psychotherapeutic Technique.* New York: Brunner/Mazel, 1983.

Miller, A. *Drama of the Gifted Child.* New York: Basic Books, 1981.

Moore, T. *Care of the Soul.* New York: HarperCollins Publishers, Inc., 1992.

Moyers, B. *Healing and the Mind.* New York: Doubleday, 1993.

Naranjo, C. *Ennea-type Structures*. Nevada City, CA: Gateways/ IDHHB, Inc., 1990.

———. *Character and Neurosis*. Nevada City, CA: Gateways/IDHHB, Inc., 1994.

Oldham, J. and Morris, L. *Personality Self-Portrait*. New York: Bantam Books, 1990.

Pagels, E. *The Gnostic Gospels*. New York: Random House, 1979.

Palmer, H. *The Enneagram*. San Francisco: HarperCollins Publishers, Inc., 1988.

Poole, W. and The Institute of Noetic Sciences. *The Heart of Healing*. Atlanta: Turner Publishing, Inc., 1993.

Riso, D. *Personality Types*. Boston: Houghton Mifflin Company, 1987.

———. *Understanding the Enneagram*. Boston: Houghton Mifflin Company, 1990.

———. *Discovering Your Personality Type*. Boston: Houghton Mifflin Company, 1992.

———. *Enneagram Transformation*. Boston: Houghton Mifflin Company, 1994.

Robinson, J., editor. *Nag Hamadi Library*. San Francisco: HarperCollins Publishers, Inc., 1978.

Rossi, E. *The Psychobiology of Mind-Body Healing*. New York: W. W. Norton & Company, Inc., 1986.

Shapiro, D. *Neurotic Styles*. New York: Basic Books, 1965.

Slip, S. *Object Relations*. New York: Jason Aronson, 1984.

Snelling, J. *The Buddhist's Handbook*. Rochester: Inner Traditions International, Inc., 1991.

Solomon, M. *Narcissism and Intimacy*. New York: W. W. Norton & Company, Inc., 1989.

Stettbacher, J. *Making Sense of Suffering*. New York: Penguin Books, 1993.

Stone, H. and Stone, S. *Embracing Each Other*. Novato, CA: Nataraj Publishing, 1989.

———. *Embracing Our Selves*. Novato, CA: Nataraj Publishing, 1985.

———. *Embracing Your Inner Critic*. San Francisco: HarperSanFrancisco, 1993.

Stone, S. *The Shadow King*. Novato, CA: Nataraj Publishing, 1997.

Suzuki, S. *Zen Mind, Beginner's Mind.* New York: John Weatherhill, Inc., 1970.

Sylvester, D. *The Brutality of Fact: Interviews with Francis Bacon.* New York: Thames Hudson, Inc., 1981.

Vaughn, F. *Awakening Intuition.* New York: Anchor Press, 1986.

Watts, A. *The Book.* New York: Vintage Books/Random House, 1966.

Whitfield, C. *Healing the Child Within.* Deerfield Beach, FL: Health Communications, Inc., 1987.

Winnicott, D. W. *Home Is Where We Start From.* New York: W. W. Norton & Company, 1986.

Woodman, M. *Addiction to Perfection.* Toronto: Inner City Books, 1982.

Yarbro, C. *Messages From Michael,* New York: Berkley Books, 1980.

———. *More Messages From Michael.* New York: Berkley Books, 1986.

———. *Michael's People.* New York: Berkley Books, 1988.

Index

addictions, 18, 106, 130
Adult Children of Alcoholics
    (ACA), 143
African bush, xiii, 85
Alcoholics Anonymous (AA),
    132-135
altar, 160, 165
ambition, 31, 32, 75, 76, 107, 120,
    165
attitude adjustments, 86
autonomy, 3, 105, 108, 165, 169

Backlash, the, 16, 108, 165
Backslide, the, 17, 18, 99, 108,
    110, 113, 120, 166
Bacon, Francis, 119
balance, 5, 98, 99
    play, 100, 101, 107
    rest, 100, 101, 107
    study, 100, 107
    work, 99, 107
    of work, study, rest, and play,
        99, 101
beginning again, 108
beginning where you are, 89, 118
blind spots, 14, 15, 162
body signals, 50, 94, 142, 148
Borderline Personality Disorder
    (BPD), 2, 167
breaking rules, 108
breathing, 112, 113

career, 10, 11, 123-125, 127, 128
change, 17, 20, 21, 31, 68, 74, 90
Chronic Fatigue Immune Dys-
    function Syndrome (CFIDS),
    51
collapse, 3-5, 16, 49, 110, 126, 165,
    167
coming into the moment, 97, 98
"community within," the, 126
compassion, 6, 7, 116, 118, 119
crying, 103, 104
curiosity, 22, 92-94, 104, 105, 118

dark side, 95, 166
death urge, 8, 17
denial, 67, 106
depression, 5-7, 14, 16, 18, 58, 66,
    67, 72, 93, 99, 104, 110, 112,
    167
disguises, 115, 166
dream work, 114, 115
dreams, 24, 114

essence, 20, 23, 162
Essence (the soul), 27, 37, 87, 94,
    113, 115, 166
excellence, 62, 76, 167

fair witness, 104, 105, 114, 142
false self, 2, 88

fear, 3, 18, 19, 21, 29, 37-40, 43,
    44, 46-50, 69, 75, 87, 88, 112,
    115, 123, 124
    of change, 42

Gandhi, Mahatma, 24, 119
Grim Reaper, The, 70, 75
guilt, 34, 35, 108, 166

heart work, 118, 119, 167
Helpless, 5, 6, 8, 9, 16, 17, 25, 26,
    33, 34, 99, 112, 113, 167
helpless role, 2
helplessness, 2, 3, 159
human needs, 105, 106
humor, 30, 31, 102, 103

idealism, 32, 167
injury, 4, 27, 37
    specific areas of, 3
inner guidance, 7, 71
Inner Guidance (soul wisdom), 16,
    23, 25-30, 35, 73, 85-88,
    90-94, 97, 105, 113-116, 167
    Asking Session, 161, 163
    course, 71, 153
    in daily life, 24
    in emergencies, 26
    group mirroring, 159, 163
    "state of the union," the, 161
    Writing Session, 154, 163
internal conflict, 15

jerks, 89, 96

law of cause and effect, the, 98, 99,
    107
life and career, 9
life force, 8, 17, 110, 113, 120
listening, 93, 94
listening within, 25

loss, accepting, 88

master of disguises, 28
meditation, 112-114
mindfulness, 92, 108
Mirror Exercise, 161
mirroring, 26, 168

narcissism, 2
need, 102, 103
needs, 105, 106
No-Agreement Exercise, the, 126

obsession, 28, 29, 89, 168

peak performers, 125
perfectionism, 2, 3, 7, 8, 35, 37,
    168
    consequences of, 13, 18
    in others, 79-83
    predicament of, 5
    recovery from, 77, 85, 88, 103
    selective, 4
perfectionism, stories of
    Doug, 143-150
    Florence, 135-138
    Jennifer, 143, 144, 146-150
    Jillian, 130-132
    Kathy, 132-135
    Michael, 138-140
    Patricia, 141-143
perfectionism, types of
    Arrogance, 38, 39, 165
    Greed-Envy, 48, 49, 132, 166
    Image Vanity, 40, 42, 167
    Impatience, 44, 46, 167
    Martyrdom, 43, 44, 168
    Righteousness, 46, 47, 169
    Self-Deprecation, 39, 40, 169
    Self-Destruction, 49, 50, 169
    Stubbornness, 42, 43, 170

psychoneuroimmunology, 19, 168

Ram Dass, 16, 112
real self, 13, 89, 92
Rebel, The, 33, 169
relationships, 4, 34, 89, 101, 130
reparenting, 116-118, 169
responsibility, 33, 34

self-acceptance, 7, 13, 20, 21, 88,
    90, 96, 129
self-care, 16, 21, 34, 49-51, 106,
    107
self-discipline, 107, 108
self-mastery, 33, 125
self-mirroring, 109
self-talk, 93, 108
spiritual work, 120
struggle, 8, 9, 127, 128
suffering, 92

support, 27, 101, 102, 107, 121
support system, 24
surrender, 110

Trickster, The, 30, 31, 170
true nature, 14, 15
twelve-step work, 134

unconscious, the, 25, 111, 116, 129,
    163

void, the, 110, 113, 115, 116

whining, 102, 103

Zen Buddhism, 23
Zen meditation, 113, 140, 142

Cynthia Curnan, Ph.D., is a psychotherapist in private practice in Los Angeles. She received her doctorate in psychology from Ryokan College, where her studies focused on inner guidance and the problems associated with perfectionism. Continuing that focus today, she specializes in work with creative people who lead highly stressful lives, counseling clients throughout the country, facilitating Inner Guidance courses, and leading Sacred Wilderness Retreats for women. She is also an artist, lecturer, and world traveler, who describes herself as a "recovering perfectionist." Her loves, she notes, include "a wonderful man, my son Chris, my grandson Hoku, nature, beauty, animals, and laughter."

Readers desiring to learn more about Cynthia and her work are invited to visit her World Wide Web site at http://www.ccurnan.com.

Other outstanding books from North Star Publications

DANCING IN THE DARK
The Shadow Side of Intimate Relationships
Douglas & Naomi Moseley

"A+✓ [TOP RATING]. This book is not for the faint-hearted, but it is for those who want to take their relationship to a glorious level—and are willing to do the work in the shadows to get there."
— *Marriage Magazine*

"Bravo! Brava! Finally a book with real solutions for real relationships...a must-read for individuals, couples, and helping professionals."
— Pat Love, Ed.D., co-author of *Hot Monogamy*

"I highly recommend this amazing book. The Moseleys' concepts are new and revolutionary. They have changed me personally and have altered the way I work with my patients."
— Jane Myers Drew, Ph.D., author of
Where Were You When I Needed You, Dad?

SOUL PLAY
Turning Your Daily Dramas into Divine Comedies
Vivian King, Ph.D.

"High drama and deep soul join in this profound and powerful journey. One discovers oneself as a player on the stage of the world, a co-creator in the theatre of the mind."
— Jean Houston, Ph.D., Director, The Foundation for Mind Research

"Who would have thought a self-help book could be so much fun and so profoundly impactful at the same time. I highly recommend *Soul Play* to those committed to taking charge of their lives."
— Jack Canfield, co-author of *Chicken Soup for the Soul*

"*Soul Play* presents an entertaining and effective way to discover, develop, and integrate the many archetypal energies that exist within us all."
— Shakti Gawain, author of *Creative Visualization* and *Living in the Light*

FISHING BY MOONLIGHT
The Art of Choosing Intimate Partners
Colene Sawyer, Ph.D.

Winner: 1997 Clark Vincent Award from the California Association of Marriage and Family Therapists.

"From healing past pain to preparing for a heathy mate, this book is filled with useful insights."
— John Gray, Ph.D., author of
  Men Are From Mars, Women Are From Venus

"...well-written, practical...a love guide I can recommend without hesitation ...delightfully honest..."
— San Jose Mercury News

"...a 'Must Read' for everyone who wants to have a meaningful relationship, whatever the stage of their relationship...you need to read and devour Fishing by Moonlight."
— Living Solo Magazine

SPIRITUALITY
Where Body and Soul Encounter the Sacred
Carl McColman

"Spirituality provides multiple doorways of comfort and insight...a practical book for personal, professional, and deep interior exploration."
— Angeles Arrien, Ph.D., Cultural Anthropologist, author of
  The Four-Fold Way and Signs of Life

"Carl McColman writes from within a clear religious tradition, but in a way which is open and accessible to people who are struggling with what they can believe. His book will be of great help to many people."
— Kenneth Leech, author of Soul Friend and True Prayer

"This book can befriend all who are walking their spiritual journey, whether they are just beginning or walking down the road a bit."
— Mary Reuter, O.S.B., Ph.D., Associate Professor of Theology
  College of Saint Benedict, St. Joseph, MN